THE ANCHORED LIFE

ADVANCE PRAISE

"I have never spent much time on boats, but I have learned so much about boating and practical insights for Christian living from *The Anchored Life*. It is rich with sailing images interwoven with Scripture and life. For me, the book's highlight was the image of the prophets being carried along by the wind of the Holy Spirit" (2 Peter 2:21). The challenging question for me is, "How do we set sail and allow the Spirit to be our Propulsion?" I encourage you to be propelled by the Spirit as you read *The Anchored Life*."

Paul L. King, Th.D., D.Min.
Author of *Genuine Gold*

"I know very little about navigation. I didn't take it seriously when I first began reading this book, *The Anchored Life: Nautical Principles that Help Believers Grow*. I thought it was a kid-friendly satire of the truth. My views began to change as I read the book. I may not be nautically literate, but as I read the book, I began to see that it was more significant than I had first thought. I read this book enough to see how it could influence people. The last section of questions is the most important element of each chapter. This book would be suitable for individual Bible study, small-group Bible study, or even a church study for the local congregation. The questions at the end of each chapter are essential for the reader to reflect on what they have just read and how it relates to them personally as Christians. This book will have a significant impact on a lot of people."

Dr. James L. Snyder
Author of the best-selling book *In Pursuit of God: The Life of A.W. Tozer*

"This inspired me to sail through life with a new attitude, realizing life is all about how you navigate the ups and downs."

Mat O'Neill
CEO, *The Adventure Buddies*

"There are few allegorical pictures that represent navigating the Christian life better than seafaring. Offering our lives as living sacrifices in practical service is an individual and community function that has many parallels in all that is required for men and women to maintain and run a taught ship. Therefore, I cannot recommend *The Anchored Life* enough for its comprehensive unpacking of nautical themes and terminology to help us better participate in our own spiritual formation in order to serve as Christ's body."

Rev. John Klobuchar
Custody Chaplain and Retired Coast Guard Master Chief, MDIV.

"This was an outstanding book that gave me flashbacks to when I was a Seaman on a U.S. Navy destroyer for over three years where we weathered two hurricanes and one typhoon. There were times when I didn't think we would survive the storms. I can understand the great fear of the Apostles when the Sea of Galilee was tossing their small craft up, down, and sideways (Matt. 8: 23-27). I believe the Lord can still the waters in the storms of our lives today as He did then—we just need to ask Him."

Dave Cavill
Seaman 1st Class, USNR 1967

"In a wonderfully creative way, Tim Hibsman and Marvin Nelson use nautical themes to illuminate God's Word and navigate the reader on a course of Christian growth and healing. This refreshing book is practical, easy to read, and enjoyable. This will be a valuable resource for every church's discipleship program."

Ron Walborn
Dean of Alliance University and Alliance Theological Seminary
New York City

"*The Anchored Life* is a powerful analogy using an old sailing vessel to teach powerful truths of our personal walk with the Lord. The person who takes the time to prayerfully answer the questions found in the book will grow in their intimacy with Jesus Christ, and their experience of the freedom we have in Him will become a reality."

Bradley R. Sickler
Captain, Chaplain Corps, United States Navy Reserve (Retired)

"What an inspirational book! Doesn't matter the path you are on, God our Captain will always redirect us and give us a detour. Just watch your navigational Beacon!"

Trevi O'Neill
President of The Adventure Buddies

Nautical Principles that Help Believers Grow

THE ANCHORED LIFE

TIM HIBSMAN AND MARV NELSON

Ambassador International
GREENVILLE, SOUTH CAROLINA & BELFAST, NORTHERN IRELAND

www.ambassador-international.com

THE ANCHORED LIFE
Nautical Principles that Help Believers Grow
©2023 Tim Hibsman and Marv Nelson
All rights reserved

ISBN: 978-1-64960-583-2, hardcover
ISBN: 978-1-64960-379-1, paperback
eISBN: 978-1-64960-383-8

Cover Design by Hannah Linder Designs
Interior Typesetting by Dentelle Design
Edited by Katie Cruice Smith

No part of this publication may be reproduced, distributed, or transmitted in any form or by any means, including photocopying, recording, or other electronic or mechanical methods, without the prior written permission of the publisher, except in the case of brief quotations embodied in critical reviews and certain other noncommercial uses permitted by copyright law. For permission requests, contact the publisher using the information below.

Royalty-free clipart obtained from: https://publicdomainvectors.org

Peter Jackson, director. *The Lord of the Rings: The Fellowship of the Ring*. Burbank: New Line Cinema, 2001. 2 hours, 58 minutes.

Peter Jackson, director. *The Lord of the Rings: The Two Towers*. Burbank: New Line Cinema, 2002. 2 hours, 59 minutes.

Peter Jackson, director. *The Lord of the Rings: The Return of the King*. Burbank: New Line Cinema, 2003. 3 hours, 30 minutes.

AMBASSADOR INTERNATIONAL
Emerald House
411 University Ridge, Suite B14
Greenville, SC 29601
United States
www.ambassador-international.com

AMBASSADOR BOOKS
The Mount
2 Woodstock Link
Belfast, BT6 8DD
Northern Ireland, United Kingdom
www.ambassadormedia.co.uk

The colophon is a trademark of Ambassador, a Christian publishing company.

INTRODUCTION

Life is a journey. As Christians, we have set sail on a journey of worship, service, and evangelism. We are not sitting around stagnantly waiting for experiences. The Christian life has a purpose and a clear destination. We know our purpose and objectives from both Scripture and the Spirit. Our journey is also a process, and that process is full of learning opportunities. The following book compares the Christian journey to nautical and maritime principles. The comparison should enlighten the reader to visualize the Christian concepts in a more focused and clear perspective and understanding.

The Christian journey is not for the faint of heart. It is full of storms, difficulties, and growth. The goal is to anchor all of who we are in Christ. He is our Destination. He is our Shore. He is our Lighthouse.

Throughout Scripture, we see our lives being compared to nautical principles. Within these terms, there are also principles. Wonderful, pictorial maritime principles fill the pages of Scripture. They are a wealth of knowledge. These principles put into view a way of life but also give answers to the believer on a journey. Whether you are a wayward follower or a long-time warrior in the faith, this book and these nautical principles will help grow you in your faith and give you a better sense on how to anchor your life in Christ.

When setting sail on an adventure, there are many parallels to the rewarding experiences of a Christian. There are all kinds of inspiring and creative sayings related to this journey, such as

- It's not the ship; it's the attitude and skillfulness of the sailor.
- Don't wait for the wind to change; adjust your sails and course.
- Ships in port are safe, but that is not their purpose.
- Life is a shipwreck, but remember to sing in the lifeboat.
- Anchor yourself to someone special.
- One cannot discover new oceans unless they have the courage to lose sight of land.
- Seas (seize) the day!

The key word to remember throughout this book is *connection*. There is a clear connection or relationship between nautical concepts and Christian living. You may not be the captain of a ship, but you might be the master and commander of your home. Most of us are very familiar with taking orders from someone, such as a boss, parent, spouse, captain, OOD (Officer of the Deck), or COB (Chief of the Boat, enlisted). A lookout looks for danger on the ocean, but we are all lookouts when it comes to the safety of ourselves and our loved ones. Consider the associations and links between the nautical and Christian lifestyles as you read through the concepts and Bible verses.

For centuries, a sea captain has always held a certain amount of respect. Whether it is a twenty-foot sloop or a two-thousand-foot ocean liner, the captain maintains many of the same leadership qualities. The corporate world is constantly comparing itself to nautical themes. "I'm the captain of my destiny." "Batten down the hatches." "Prepare for rough seas." "Cannot see the horizon." There are many others that embody the long history and importance of leadership and the sea.

An effective sea captain needs to keep in mind that he/she is constantly dealing with different types of groups. Therefore, the captain needs to be aware of audience analysis. One captain would give detailed speeches to officers, but to the crew, he would shorten them and make them easy to remember. One of the techniques the captain used was a clear and concise review of what he had just said. This was called takeaways. If you remembered nothing else, try to remember the takeaways so you can use the principles later. One section below implements the key takeaway principles in each topic.

As you proceed through this book, consider how you could use it to be a better leader, follower, and supporter. Utilize the key takeaways as launching pads to maintain the heading of a life securely anchored in Christ!

PART 1
THE VESSEL—YOU AND YOUR SOUL

Every sailor needs a ship to carry them out on their journey. Every believer has a vessel for this journey. The vessel may appear to be a single, solid object. In reality, it is very flexible and has many dynamic parts. Each part is distinct and provides a unique purpose.

The vessel is you—your soul and your life. Without the vessel, a journey cannot be undertaken. Scripture is full of descriptions of how we need to have a healthy vessel. When our vessel (or soul) is healthy, the journey goes better in many ways; the seas are smoother; and the storms become easier to navigate.

I (Marv) have lived at times with an unhealthy soul, and it caused me to stumble in my journey. My vessel was weighed down, full of cracks, and lost speed because many barnacles were cropping up, causing drag. I remember one time when I had allowed jealousy to cloud my ability to do ministry well. I was pastoring a college church at the University of Pittsburgh at the time. We had a healthy ministry, and God was showing up in mighty ways.

Not too long after we got started, a bigger, better, and flashier church showed up on the scene. For years, I allowed bitterness to cloud my heart and mind. Finally, I was so unhealthy that I remember tearing down all the other church's advertisements! They were advertising their church so people could come closer to Christ, and I was tearing their advertisements down! There was something clearly wrong with my soul.

Not only did this unhealthiness within my soul hurt my personal walk, I know for a fact it also hindered my leadership in my church. My bitterness leaked onto my student leadership team. We all looked at this other church with suspicion and frustration. We refused to play nice with them and even took to bashing them to others.

When we have cracks in our souls, the enemy will find ways to exploit those cracks. Just like water will find its way into a leaky vessel, the enemies' lies and schemes will find their way into a leaky soul. We need to seek the Holy Spirit to answer the question, where are the cracks in my soul? He will answer, and then we must allow Him to do His patchwork to our vessel.

As we continue to look at the real-life connection of maritime imagery, we will see different areas in our lives where the Holy Spirit may be pointing out some cracks, heaviness, or barnacles that decrease speed. These different parts of the vessel could be where the enemy is seeking to sneak his way into our souls with his lies, temptations, and manipulations. The first part of the vessel we will look at is the hull.

CHAPTER 1
THE HULL

The main base or the biggest section is the hull. The size and classification of the ship is usually determined by the length and depth of the hull. This is where the most time is spent and where there is usually a personal interaction. Crew quarters and bunks are the most private places a sailor is going to find on the ship.

The deeper the draft, the slower the ship is going to cut through the water. The draft, size of the cargo hold, and buoyancy of the ship are extremely important. If the ship is heavily laden with gold bullion, then you might have to deal with it. To avoid being too heavy, the ballast is often discarded and replaced with heavy cargo to maximize the weight of the ship. Also, if the hull is covered with barnacles, the speed will be greatly reduced.

When we look at our souls, the hull is one of the most important places to look for cracks, weight, or drag. A few questions of assessment are key. Do we have cracks in our hull? If so, can those be patched, or do we need to go to port and renew the hull? What weight is in our hull that is too heavy or out of balance, thereby slowing our progress? What barnacles are attached to our hull that are making our vessel sluggish?

It is vital that we answer these questions for our growth and forward momentum in our walk of faith. In Psalm 139:23-24, David asks the Spirit to reveal to him these very issues. "Search me, O God, and know my heart! Try me and know my thoughts! And see if there be any grievous way in me, and lead me in the way everlasting!" David recognized he needed the

Spirit's help seeing the cracks, weight, and drag. He also recognized his need of the Lord's help to deal with those issues.

Cracks can and will appear with neglect. If we neglect to seek the Lord's face, we can easily allow the enemy to make and exploit the cracks in our soul. Sin patterns will begin to appear. Lack of desire for the Lord and His will are certain to show up. Being on our knees, spending time with the Lord, and daily taking up our cross are keys to the maintenance of our hull.

The causes of cracks can be legion, but I have experienced that the cracks often show up in our hull from these six sources of weight and drag: past pain, ungrieved losses, unforgiveness, family sin patterns, unconfessed sin, and the acceptance of lies about one's identity or God's identity.[1]

THE WEIGHT OF PAST PAIN

To be human is to experience pain, and we have all experienced it in the past and will in the future. Pain cannot be ignored, but many believers do just that. Our past pain has the power to predict our current realities if we do not deal with them properly. The pain of my last broken relationship will invade my new, developing relationship. The woundedness of my parental hurt will invade my marriage or the way I parent. These past pains will invade our current realities unless we fully deal with past pain.

Just like the hull of a ship needs maintenance, so does our soul. Pain brings stress to our souls and keeps us off balance, like a ship without the right ballast. When we live with a lens focused on our past pains, we only see pain ahead on our headings. We lose hope, and we lose heart. Pain brings with it a sense of loss, and so we need to evaluate our past pain. Have you been allowing the pains of yesterday to hinder your life of today? If so, do some hull maintenance, with the guidance of the Holy Spirit, so you can be balanced once again.

---

[1] Dr. Rob Reimer, *Soul Care: 7 Transformational Principles for a Healthy Soul* (Franklin: Carpenter's Son Publishing, 2016).

THE WEIGHT OF UNGRIEVED LOSS

Another main crack in the hull of many souls is the presence of ungrieved loss. Jesus tells us in His famous Sermon on the Mount, "'Blessed are those who mourn, for they shall be comforted'" (Matt. 5:4). The inverse is true then: we cannot receive comfort unless we first mourn or grieve. Like past pain, ungrieved loss will weigh us down and throw us off balance. These two heavy issues can even go hand in hand. When we neglect to properly grieve the losses in life, we bottle up those emotions and continually carry their heavy weight. When we do this, our hull can only take so much loss before it breaks.

One mentor always taught me to think of it as a beachball. No matter how hard we shove a beachball under water, it will *always* pop back up, and we will not be able to control where it appears. Our losses are the same. Ungrieved losses can create "triggers" in our lives. For example, if your parent called you a liar all your life, this is a loss of identity. This loss, ungrieved and undealt with, will make you more susceptible to flying off the handle at someone who insinuates you are being deceptive. The pain/loss happened as a child, but as an adult, you cannot help but revert to your inner child when you react.

My ungrieved loss of never measuring up to my father created within me a people-pleaser lifestyle. I felt as if I needed to earn the love of those around me by making sure they were constantly pleased. I remember the moment I realized how bad my people-pleasing was. I was tasked by my boss to head to the store to pick up some chips. I went to the store, got to the chip aisle, and froze. *What if I get the wrong chips? What if I spend too much money?* I had to call and ask him to tell me what chips to buy, so I did not displease him with the wrong ones.

That story is ridiculous, and most people don't struggle as deeply with people-pleasing as I did, but there are other cracks in your hull that need healing and patching. What are the losses in your life that you know you have not properly grieved?

THE WEIGHT OF UNFORGIVENESS

One of the things we must all come to grips with is that no one goes through life without being wounded by another person. One way or another, we will be hurt by someone, and we will hurt someone. When people wound us, this can put a crack in our hull and hinder our souls. Yet if we allow that wound to fester with the balloon of unforgiveness, our hull may be so cracked, it allows the whole ship to sink.

Unforgiveness creates bitterness. Bitterness creates a deep darkness within one's soul. When we withhold forgiveness, we are not hurting the other person; we are hurting ourselves. That person controls the rudder to our lives. We hand them the control willingly when we neglect to forgive them.

Corrie ten Boom, a woman with deep hurt, pain, and loss at the hands of German Nazis, once said, "Forgiveness is the key which unlocks the door of resentment and the handcuffs of bitterness."[2] Corrie ten Boom was able to live a life of courage and tell a testimony of how she had overcome because of her great forgiveness! Unforgiveness really is a trap, and it creates great holes in our hulls. A good question to ask is when I think of those who have hurt me, what feelings arise within me? Those feelings will tell you whether or not you have forgiven that person.

THE BARNACLE OF FAMILY SIN PATTERNS

Whether we know it or not, we all inherit family patterns—for good or for ill. Sometimes, these family patterns are familial sins that are passed down from generation to generation. Over time, these sin patterns cause greater and greater cracking in the hull of the next generation. Patterns

---

2   Corrie ten Boom and Jamie Buckingham, *Tramp for the Lord* (Fort Washington: CLC Publications, 2010), 52.

may include divorce, abuse, sexual addiction, alcoholism, rejection, anger, drug use, secrecy, adultery, gambling, or even favoritism.

The real danger in these patterns is the acceptance of them. We saw our father live this way, so we chalked it up to "It's just the way I am." That's like looking at a crack on the hull of a boat that could pop any moment into a giant hole and saying, "Well, that crack is just a part of the hull now; let's go on a long trip and do nothing about it!" or "Wow, that giant barnacle is really hindering our speed—that's just the way the ocean is, I guess!" That sounds ridiculous because it is.

If we do not name, label, deal with, and repent of family sin patterns, not only will we allow the cracks to remain in our own souls and the barnacles on our hulls to remain, but we will also pass that brokenness on to the next generation and cause them to start life with cracks in their souls and barnacles on their hulls that need not be there. Dealing with these can be extremely painful. In order to do so, you *must* ask the Holy Spirit to guide and direct you. Find a good Spirit-filled friend to help you walk through these as well. Do not neglect to deal with these cracks in the soul.

THE WEIGHT OF UNCONFESSED SIN

As a believer, you already know the importance of repentance. We often have this sense, like Adam and Eve in the Garden, that God is going to shame us or turn away from us if we come and confess our sins. We sin, and we run. Often, this pattern finds its way into our normal interaction with the Lord. But what did the Lord say to Adam and Eve? Genesis 3:9-10 reads, "But the Lord God called to the man and said to him, 'Where are you?' And he said, 'I heard the sound of you in the garden, and I was afraid, because I was naked, and I hid myself.'" God pursued them. He called out to them and asked where they were! When we sin, the Lord desires we run *to* Him, not *from* Him!

What are the areas of secret sin in your life? What sins do you think are so dark that you keep them completely hidden from your spouse, your friends, yourself, and your God? He knows it exists. Nothing surprises God. It is not as if you will confess your mess to Him and He will shout from Heaven, "Gasp! I never knew you struggled with this!" No, He knows. He knew why Adam hid, and He even knew where Adam was hiding! Yet God lovingly pursued after Adam and Eve and brought them back into relationship.

As a ministry major at a Christian college, I struggled heavily with pornography. I hid it, buried it, and continued to nurse my sin in secret. Porn comforted me (or so I thought). I felt in control. Yet deep within me, I knew I had to give it up. All of those feelings were illusions! I was being eaten alive with guilt and shame. I did not want to be rejected by God, my college, my friends, or my girlfriend (who is now my wife). Yet one day, I confessed. I let it all out there with my friend Ben, and my life has never been the same!

As a pastor, when times get rough, I struggle with overeating. There are times when I gain a ton of weight. In the end, though, I feel the still, small voice of the Lord convincing me to confess my hidden sins. This allows the Spirit to patch up my cracked hull. My sailing with Him goes so much smoother when the hull is repaired. Let go of your secret sins and allow Him to heal the cracks in your soul.

THE BARNACLE OF IDENTITY LIES

The enemy's greatest "hull-breaker" comes in the form of broken identity. He will try to break your identity and the identity of the Lord. He will try to push you down with lies of who you are and Who God is. With unconfessed sin, he will say things to you like, "That's too messed up. You're no good. Don't tell anyone; don't confess it because you'll be shown for who you really are—a screw up!"

These lies fester, and soon, we begin to believe the lies the enemy spews about us. He will lie about Who God is. He will say God could never love you. He will besmirch the name of God in your heart, but we must not let him!

One huge identity wound in my life was and is rejection. This has been an issue and a wound for a long time in my life and has taken many different forms, and I have felt it in different ways over the years. Reading through *Soul Care* again with the lens of "where's the rejection" helped reframe a lot of the teaching to help me wrestle with rejection in a way that has been helpful. In discussing identity, wounds, family sin patterns, and forgiveness, *Soul Care* hit directly on the issue of rejection.

I have found myself seeking to build my identity on what I can do and how I can perform. When navigating life in this way, if I received praise, I felt I had succeeded. When I was seemingly ignored, I felt rejection and chalked it up to "I am not good enough."

I would see a mentor praise another person for something great they had done or a book they had written or a sermon they had preached and found myself feeling rejected because they had never done that to or for me. I would find myself jealous and feeling rejected when another mentor was in a "small group of pastors" that met every month, and I was not in it, but another person I knew was.

These issues stirred rejection within me. Typing that out makes it sound so lame, but that is because the lie of rejection causes us to be petty and creates a subtle immaturity of jealousy within a person through the dangerous act of comparison.

I have also discovered that this issue of rejection is a familial pattern. In one way or another, the siblings on my dad's side (including my dad) felt rejected. Whether they felt this from their mom (my nana) or their dad (my papa), the wounds went deep. I know for a fact my mother has wrestled with the self-same issue as well. Rejection is more than a word or feeling in my family; it is a disease that has caused many of us Nelsons to be performance-based people-pleasers.

In *Soul Care*, Rob Reimer says, "We shield our wounds, and we normalize our wounds and our shielding."[3] Performance has been a shield to my rejection wound, and I have spent decades normalizing it. I have pushed myself many times to be "successful" in order to shield the rejection wound. I cared about the adulation and praise from those I looked up to more so than really resting in the acceptance of the Father.

Where has the enemy been busting up the hull of your soul with lies about who you are and about Who God is? Where have you been carrying a load not your own? Ask the Spirit of the Lord to speak truth into you—into your heart and into your soul—so you can get those holes patched up, and you can continue to maintain the heading the Lord has given specifically to you.

Like the hull, every Christian needs a firm foundation to get started. The foundation of Christianity states that there is one God Who is infinitely perfect, existing eternally in three Persons—Father, Son, and Holy Spirit. Jesus died on the cross as a substitutionary sacrifice, and all who believe in Him are justified on the grounds of His shed blood. Salvation has been provided through Jesus Christ for all men, and those who repent and believe in Him are born again of the Holy Spirit, receive the gift of eternal life, and become the children of God.

KEY TAKEAWAY PRINCIPLES

- It is important to have a firm foundation and stable platform.
- Take care of maintenance (barnacles).
- Draft equals clearance and speed.
- Ballast slows the ship down but creates stability.

FURTHER STUDY

- "But when the goodness and loving kindness of God our Savior appeared, he saved us, not because of works done by us in

---

3   *Soul Care*, p. 134.

righteousness, but according to his own mercy, by the washing of regeneration and renewal of the Holy Spirit, whom he poured out on us richly through Jesus Christ our Savior, so that being justified by his grace we might become heirs according to the hope of eternal life" (Titus 3:4-7).

- "'Go therefore and make disciples of all nations, baptizing them in the name of the Father and of the Son and of the Holy Spirit, teaching them to observe all that I have commanded you. And behold, I am with you always, to the end of the age'" (Matt. 28:19-20).
- "(We were in all 276 persons in the ship.)" (Acts 27:37).
- "And when they had eaten enough, they lightened the ship, throwing out the wheat into the sea" (Acts 27:38).
- "Then the mariners were afraid, and each cried out to his god. And they hurled the cargo that was in the ship into the sea to lighten it for them. But Jonah had gone down into the inner part of the ship and had lain down and was fast asleep" (Jonah 1:5).

CHAPTER 2
DECK

Every sailor knows how slippery a wooden deck can be when it gets wet. The mist and waves of the ocean, combined with the angle of the moving ship, can make the deck a hard place to stand. The crew must work in this environment. Sometimes, it is so dangerous that the crew will wear safety harnesses. Sometimes, crew members work in pairs and help each other. Four hands or four feet may be better than two.

As we continue to liken the image of a boat to our soul, what would possibly make the deck of our souls wet? We think it would be temptation. Temptation wets the deck, making choices in your life slippery. Temptation splashes water on the deck of the soul, hoping that you will fall and be unable to properly sail the ship.

Trying to stand on a wet deck, in general, is dangerous. But standing on a wet deck without being rigged to something in the middle of a storm is just plain stupid. Yet, as believers, we often entertain temptation and allow our deck to get quite wet and slippery. When storms come against our lives, we struggle to right the ship or maintain course because we have entertained our temptations too long. We have allowed those thoughts and fleshly desires to soak the deck of our souls.

Temptation can be difficult to navigate; but in the book of James, we read about how to deal with, understand, and flee temptation. James 1:14-15 explains how temptation works: "But each person is tempted when he is lured and enticed by his own desire. Then desire when it has conceived gives birth to sin, and sin when it is fully grown brings forth death."

A great key in cleaning up the deck of our soul lies within this short passage. Temptation is essentially the enemy using our fleshly desires against us. The enemy knows where we are weak and purposefully puts things, thoughts, or people in our path who are going to entice those fleshly desires within us. Satan does not create the desires; he puts the water on the deck, hoping we will slip up and give in.

This is an important realization because this Scripture shows us the source of the wet deck—our flesh! We must seek to ask the Spirit to purify our desires, cleanse our hearts, and give us the ability to reject our flesh. This tethers us to the truth and helps us navigate the wet deck without falling. When the enemy shows up to entice our flesh, we will not *want* to give into it because we will have allowed the Spirit to remove the desire to fall prey to that enticement. When we ask the Spirit to search us, we will find those areas of fleshly desire and seek to bring them under the Lordship of Christ. Also, the more time we spend in the presence of the Lord, the less we will be prone to sin. Our desire will move from pleasing ourselves to pleasing Him alone.

James also gives great insight into how we can get out of moments of temptation when we have allowed ourselves to get enticed. He says, "Submit yourselves therefore to God. Resist the devil, and he will flee from you. Draw near to God, and he will draw near to you. Cleanse your hands, you sinners, and purify your hearts, you double-minded" (James 4:7-8).

When we have dropped our guard and given our flesh a foothold, we have a moment of decision before we move forward in the sin by which we have become overwhelmingly enticed. We have a retreat. We have the presence of the Lord. If we remain in His presence, we will not want to give into the flesh; but when we fall prey and are on the cusp of giving into the temptation on the deck of our souls, we can once again turn to Him. We can draw near to Him. This, in effect, tethers us to the Lord like sailors tether themselves to one another in order to not slip on a wet deck. He is the Tether we need in times of temptation.

The key in those moments of edge-stepping temptation is submission. When we feel the Lord calling us away from the ledge, we must go with Him. We need to heed the voice of the Lord calling us back and draw near to Him. The *only* way we can resist the devil in these moments is submission and resistance.

A while back, I had one of those edge-stepping moments. I heard some news that a person in leadership in our college church was considering leaving our church and was, in fact, attending another church. I felt a deep sadness come over me. I love this person. Why would they "betray me" in this way? I wrestled through it and thought I was okay.

When I got home, I wanted to eat my feelings, as I so often have done. I wanted to nurse my wounds. Right when I was feeling this tug, I felt the Spirit draw me back. It was like an alert from a ship's collision warning. I heard the Spirit say, "You do not want to eat that way." And I found myself saying, "I do not want to eat that way!" It was *great* to then draw near to the Lord. I did not eat that way.

What is the big idea then? First, seek to dry the deck of your soul. One of my favorite questions that is often asked of people seeking licensure in our denomination is from our district superintendent. He asks, "If the enemy were to derail you in your ministry, where would he attack?" This is a perfect question to ask ourselves. So, we must ask the Spirit to reveal those areas of our lives that can be enticed by the enemy to draw us into sin. Seek His cleansing power. Pursue His presence to dry that out of your life.

The next thing we need to do is heed the voice of the Lord when we have allowed our deck to get a little slippery and flee from the devil. When we draw near to the Light, the Prince of Darkness will have to flee! Dry that deck, sailors! Having a firm footing is a blessing.

KEY TAKEAWAY PRINCIPLES

- Make sure you have a firm foothold.
- Take extra precautions when there is a slippery deck or other obstacles.
- Sometimes, you may have to ask for help.

FURTHER STUDY

- "Teach me to do your will, for you are my God! Let your good Spirit lead me on level ground" (Psalm 143:10).
- "He drew me up from the pit of destruction, out of the miry bog, and set my feet upon a rock, making my steps secure" (Psalm 40:2).
- "You therefore, beloved, knowing this beforehand, take care that you are not carried away with the error of lawless people and lose your own stability" (2 Peter 3:17).

CHAPTER 3
SAILS AND PROPULSION

The optimum situation is to always be moving toward a brighter, better, and more profitable horizon. That is hard to do if you are sitting dead in the water, not moving. Modern ships have engines to propel them through the water. In the past, there were other methods of propulsion. The Romans and Phoenicians often utilized oars and manpower. The cheaper and less reliable source was the wind.

The more sail or square footage of canvas means more speed. But it also means more weight and more manpower to maintain. There are all kinds of sails for different purposes designed to create the maximum amount of speed. Some examples include mainsail, head sail/flying jib, genoa, spinnaker, and gennaker. Sometimes, the wind is so strong that the sails come under extreme pressure, and they could actually tear—especially if they are older, weathered material.

We all have sails and wind propelling our lives. What motivates us? What gets us up in the morning? Whose agenda are we waking up to tackle day in and day out? The answer to those questions would be a good indicator as to what is putting wind in our sails and propelling us forward in life.

In Scripture, we see the Holy Spirit often likened to the wind. In 2 Peter 1:21, we read, "For no prophecy was ever produced by the will of man, but men spoke from God as they were carried along by the Holy Spirit." That phrase "carried along" is actually a nautical phrase where the Spirit is seen as directing and propelling the prophets forward like a wind does a ship. The question we need to be asking as believers then is "How do we set sail and allow the Spirit to be our propulsion?"

Let us start with a story. There used to be a time when electricity was not accessible to homes. When it became available, many jumped at the chance to have this new type of power. One such person was a wealthy, elderly lady. She called the power company and asked them to install her electricity so she could have lights at night. The power company came out and did as she requested. The next month, the meter reader came to her house and noticed she had not used any noticeable power. He called the installers and sought to see if they had installed it correctly, and they declared they had.

The following month, the meter read very low numbers of usage once more. This time, the meter reader went to the elderly lady's door and knocked. When she came to the door, he explained the issue and asked if everything was working all right. She stated rather excitedly that yes, everything was in working order.

He inquired why there was such a low output, and the lady stated, "Oh. I turn on my lights at night long enough to light my candles. It was always so hard trying to track them down when the sun had gone down."

The meter reader walked away baffled. Why would she purchase the power if she was not going to tap into all of it?

Sadly, I think this is true for you and me when it comes to setting the proper sails in the boat of our lives. We have absolute access to the power of the Spirit but fail to fully access it. There are several reasons for the lack of acquisition of the Spirit's power. One of them is that Satan has caused such a fear to arise around the Person and work of the Holy Spirit. This fear has caused many pastors and churches to neglect preaching and teaching on the Holy Spirit. Ignoring the Spirit interferes with our access to God's power.

Another reason for our lack of tapping into the Spirit's power is because we believe the lie that it is only accessible to "special believers." However, the Holy Spirit is not only accessible to special people! The Spirit is part of the normal Christian life. So, we have access to the Spirit's power. Again, the question is "How do we set sail and allow the Spirit to be our propulsion?"

STUDY FIRST

Read Luke 24:49 and Acts 1:8, 2:1-4.

In these passages, we see not only the promise of the Spirit's coming and empowering, but we also see the fulfillment of this promise. This empowerment is for all who claim Christ as their Lord and Savior.

PERSONALIZE THE PROMISE OF THE SPIRIT

The first thing we must do in order to be propelled by the Spirit is to make it personal. Near the end of His life and after His resurrection, Jesus made sure the disciples knew of the coming Holy Spirit. In John chapters fourteen to sixteen, He describes what the power of the Spirit will look like and how it will manifest in their lives. He describes Who the Holy Spirit is (not what) because the Holy Spirit is a Person, just as real as you and I are.

Jesus declared to His disciples, "Nevertheless, I tell you the truth: it is to your advantage that I go away, for if I do not go away, the Helper will not come to you. But if I go, I will send him to you" (John 16:7). This, as well as all of the other promises of the Holy Spirit, were not just for the disciples but for you and me as well. Too often, we move in the spirit of religion and not in the Holy Spirit.

A.W. Tozer once said, "The great woe is not the presence of religious toys and trifles, but the necessity for them because the presence of the Eternal Spirit is not in our midst."[4] We try to do this walk alone and neglect to see we have a Helper. We try to do the "religious thing" and miss the point altogether.

Some Christians—even pastors—today would say that these promises are not for you and me. Some will even try to cause a fear of fanaticism if we own these promises. I tell you, however, we are to make these promises

---

[4] A.W. Tozer and James L. Snyder, *Tozer: The Mystery of the Holy Spirit* (Alachua: Bridge-Logos, 2007), 24.

personal. They are promises from the lips of God to the depths of our hearts. Take a hold of them like the early sailors took a hold of the ropes and raised their sails. You must own the reality that God desires to empower you. Once we have moved to the place of personalizing the promises of the Spirit, it is time to move into the next "how of propulsion."

RELEASE ANY THOUGHT OF SELF-RELIANCE

Jesus gave the disciples (and subsequently, us) a task: "Go therefore and make disciples . . . " (Matt. 28:19). Yet right before He leaves, He tells them to wait for the Holy Spirit. He was declaring that they had a mission, but they could not fulfill it on their own. He was stating they *needed* the Holy Spirit; otherwise, they would interfere with the fulfillment of the work to which He was calling them. If the disciples, who walked with Jesus, needed to wait for the Holy Spirit, how much more do we?

Operating in the Spirit brings opposition to the flesh. We must come to the place in our faith where we recognize that we are helpless without the Spirit. We need the wind of the Spirit to carry us along. Imagine a man trying to move his boat by blowing wind from his mouth into the sails. That is what it looks like when we try to rely on ourselves! This means giving up control.

Self-reliance is really all about control and rejecting dependence on the Spirit in order to rely on self. Dependence on the Spirit means we give up and surrender our control. It means giving Him control, and that can be quite frightening. We cannot make the Holy Spirit an "addition" to our Christian walk; He must be all. In order to access the fullness of the Spirit, we must give up control. Jim Cymbala once said, "The irony of Spirit-filled living is that we have to give up power in order to gain a greater power."[5]

Jesus Himself lived in dependence on the Holy Spirit. He did not have to, but He chose to so we could see what a Spirit-reliant life looked like and

---

5   Jim Cymbala, *Spirit Rising: Tapping into the Power of the Holy Spirit* (Grand Rapids: Zondervan, 2014), Kindle Edition.

how it opposed a self-reliant life. He stated things like, "I only do what I see my Father doing . . . " (John 5:19). He did things like getting away to places of solitude to pray (Luke 5:16). Why would He have to pray if He was leaning into His Deity rather than his humanity? Philippians 2:6-11 states that He "did not count equality with God a thing to be grasped," but rather chose to humble Himself. If the idea of Spirit-reliance was so important that Jesus would demonstrate it, I think we should take heed and allow the truth of our inability to take root. Flesh equals mess every time.

Now that we have personalized the promise and seen the importance of spirit-reliance versus self-reliance, we can move into the third area of how to be propelled by the power of the Spirit.

GO WITH THE GUIDE

When we lean into our self-reliance, we miss the paths the Spirit has laid out for us. We try to forge our own way and assume God is blessing the path. Yet without Spirit-reliance, we will miss many things the Spirit is trying to reveal and will often miss the map of the sea He is using to guide us. The Scripture reveals the Spirit as the Guide to all truth. The Spirit guides us into *aletheia*—the Greek word meaning unconcealed truth. He lays it bare and causes it to make sense.

This is true of the Word as well. There are many truths we miss in Scripture because we are leaning upon our minds alone. The Bible even says that our minds cannot fathom the depths of God's Word any more than we can dive to the deepest parts of the ocean. The Spirit wrote the Word, so He alone can reveal the Word. The Bible was not meant to be simply an educational tool for memorization. It was meant to be a transformational book that changes our lives.

The Spirit alone can enliven the Word to our hearts and cause the sails of our soul to be filled. Yet we neglect to go with the Guide because it is much "safer" to know a truth rather than live it. God desires to lead each and every one of us into transformational living where we have an eternal impact on the world. This can only happen when we go with the Guide. Paul consistently encouraged all believers to walk by the Spirit.

My family always goes to the Outer Banks for vacation. My son MJ and I like to walk on the beach. When we were walking a few years ago, MJ wanted to walk in my footprints. He loves me and has a desire to be somewhat like me. This drove him to want to see if he could follow me stride for stride by placing his small foot into my prints. Once I realized what he was doing, I began to make smaller strides because his short legs were struggling to leap in my footprints. He then was able to walk with me and follow me step for step.

The same is true for the Spirit and us. This is the image Paul was trying to create when he said, "Walk by the Spirit" (Gal. 5:16). We are to seek out where the footprints of the Spirit are and step into His footprints. He will not walk too fast or with too far a stride. He will lead us and grow us from where we are to where we could be. It is His power giving us the ability to do this as well.

We are not in this alone! We do not walk the Christian life in isolation. We must, however, reject the path we were trying to forge for ourselves in order to see His footprints. We must surrender our ways to His ways. To do this, we must seek what His way is. We must spend time with Him. We must learn His voice and then choose to follow His lead. Then—and only then—can we access the power of the Holy Spirit.

The promise of the Holy Spirit is for every believer. Jesus' words to the early church are as true now as they were then. In order to do that which Christ has called us to do, we must wait, believe the promise is for us, cease to rely on ourselves, and follow His lead. When this occurs, we will see what God is doing in our midst and excitedly join Him in His work through the power of the Holy Spirit.

KEY TAKEAWAY PRINCIPLES

- Understand what keeps you moving forward.
- You are at the mercy of the wind (and God's will).

- More square footage of sail equals more speed.
- Tearing sails means understanding limitations.
- Know the importance of shape, size, and location of sails.
- Pick your sails carefully.

FURTHER STUDY

- "They also honored us greatly, and when we were about to sail, they put on board whatever we needed" (Acts 28:10).
- "Then Eliezer the son of Dodavahu of Mareshah prophesied against Jehoshaphat, saying, 'Because you have joined with Ahaziah, the Lord will destroy what you have made.' And the ships were wrecked and were not able to go to Tarshish."
- "But there the Lord in majesty will be for us a place of broad rivers and streams, where no galley with oars can go, nor majestic ship can pass" (Isa. 33:21).

CHAPTER 4
HELM/STEERING APPARATUS

The ship's wheel keeps the ship on course. The helmsman is given a heading and keeps the ship on course. Oil lamps were used at one time to light the compass to help the navigator accomplish this purpose. The ship's wheel is one of the most iconic maritime symbols. It symbolizes direction, power, responsibility, leadership, clear water/approach, and a sense of adventure.

It is important to stay on course and not to go astray. Are you at the helm? Are you conforming to the ship's guidelines and staying on course? Or is the Lord at the helm? The Christian believer gets his coordinates and guidance from God through the Bible, spiritual leaders, and prayer; but first, he needs to release his grip on the helm.

When talking about this part of the ship, we are essentially looking at who is in control of the vessel. If we liken our life and/or soul to the metaphorical ship, we need to ask whether we are willing to surrender control of the ship to the best Captain around! We previously discussed control, but the helm is the course-setter and deserves a deeper look.

I remember a time when I needed to fix my messed-up tub. Somehow, water was getting into the tub lining and making our tub like a waterbed. Every once in a while, I would drain it through the drain plug, but I just could not fix it. I caulked like crazy—still no success. Finally, I gave in and called the one man I knew who could fix it—my father-in-law. I hated giving up and surrendering to his skills, but I knew I needed to in order to get things fixed. Eventually, we fixed it and had to regrout the entire wall of the shower.

When I try to touch house projects, it does not go well. The same is true for my life. When I try to control it, it will fail. The same is true for our church. If we do not let God lead, we will make a mess every single time. Surrender is not easy. Surrender is not a normal word in the everyday American life. We are people who do not back down or surrender!

However, with things of the soul, the only way our ship is actually going to go anywhere is through surrender. We have to recognize that within ourselves, refusal to surrender boils down to control and fear. If God takes control, will we have enough money to pay our bills? What if I do not like the direction God is taking with our church? How can I reengage my control over the direction my life or the church's life is going? We do not want Him to steer the ship because we want control. The Bible continuously reminds us of our need to let Him captain the ship, grip the helm, and keep our lives on course.

If surrender of the helm is so important to staying on course and we as believers are to hand over the helm to the Lord, the question, then, is how? How can we be wise and surrender the helm of our lives and stay on course?

STUDY FIRST

Read 1 Corinthians 1:25-31, 2:14.

Paul desired to correct much of the control issues with the Corinthian church. They loved driving the ship of their own lives. Much of how they were living was out of control because they were taking charge both of their own lives and of the church. He took time to really humble them.

RECOGNIZE OUR INADEQUACY AND REALIZE HIS SUFFICIENCY

The first thing Paul instructed the Corinthian believers was to realize how inadequate they were to control the ship and to rely on the One Who knew the course. In the Corinthian church, there were both Jews and Gentiles, and there were divisions popping up throughout the church based on which person they would follow. Teachings on philosophy and wisdom moved much of their culture, and that way of living caused the church members of the Corinthian church to live prideful lives. This then caused the church members to try and be holy on their own instead of relying upon God to lead and teach them. The Corinthians desired God's power but did not desire to surrender to Him. They wanted God's blessing on them as a church, but they did not want to follow Him fully.

As followers of Christ, we must seek God's face, not just His hands. Paul then goes on to finish the first chapter with a description of just how low they (and we) are compared to God and His wisdom. The Corinthian church was living arrogantly, as if they were the best thing since sliced bread and the holiest of the holies. But Paul brought them back down to earth with his statements, especially when he says, "For the foolishness of God is wiser than men, and the weakness of God is stronger than men" (1 Cor. 1:25). This church, in its arrogance, thought their wisdom was enough.

I fear we live similarly to the Corinthian church. Many of us can make Jesus an addition to our lives, but Jesus is not an addition. He is to be our *All*. We act as if our wisdom is all we need, and God is a buddy we meet with once a week. We captain our own ship because we feel we have the ability to properly hold the helm and keep a steady course. Yet we are shown repeatedly to be inadequately trained and/or ready for such a monumental task.

The Corinthian culture upheld wisdom and philosophy as the things of utmost importance. This led to severe arrogance. When God began to do amazing things in their midst, they attributed it to themselves, rather than to God.

When God shows up, we are to point to Him, not to ourselves. Do not point to your pastor or to your elders or to your church, point to Christ! Warren Wiersbe said, "The Gospel of God's grace leaves no room for personal boasting."[6] God's grace dwarfs any accomplishments we could ever hope to have. That is

---

6   Warren W. Wiersbe, *The Bible Exposition Commentary: Matthew—Galatians*, vol. 1, (London: Victor Books, 1996), 571.

why Paul quotes from Jeremiah when he states, "Let the one who boasts, boast in the Lord." God is sufficient, while we are insufficient. God is all we need, while we in and of ourselves are inadequate. Surrendering to someone who knows better is the wisest course of action.

REST OUR FAITH IN GOD'S POWER, NOT MAN'S WISDOM

Paul then moves to the what—recognizing our inadequacy and His sufficiency—and leads us answering this question of how we become wise and surrender.

Gordon Fee says, "In every possible way, Paul has tried to show them the folly of their present fascination with wisdom, which has inherent within it the folly of self-sufficiency and self-congratulation. Even the preacher whom God used to bring them to faith had to reject self-reliance."[7] Paul, who was brilliant, purposefully chose not to preach using big words and heady philosophy so that the Spirit alone could be credited with the results. Yet the Corinthians still tried to cling to men and their teachings instead of seeing the importance of reliance on God. The Corinthians wanted their brains tickled with philosophical prose, but the Lord wanted to transform their arrogant hearts.

In American church culture, there has been too much leaning on human wisdom, too much desire for wise and persuasive words. I think this is why, like so many, I was fooled by Ravi Zacharias. His words were wise and persuasive. Many a deep-thinking atheist either turned to the truth or at least considered it more closely because of Ravi's wise and persuasive words. This was man's wisdom masquerading as God's wisdom, and very few of us had the discernment to notice the difference.

When we hold the helm of our own ship, we will hit icebergs every time. We simply are not wise sailors! The Lord is the only One with the wisdom,

---

7   Gordon D. Fee, *The First Epistle to the Corinthians* (Grand Rapids: Eerdmans Publishing Co.), Kindle Edition, 94.

forethought, and ability to correctly hold the helm. The Corinthians thought they were maintaining a good course but were too ignorant to see the icebergs into which they were steering themselves.

Tozer once said, "You see, the Holy Spirit rules out and excludes all Adam's flesh, all human brightness, all that scintillating human personality, human ability and human efficiency."[8] We are to be a people of surrender and dependence, not self-reliance.

I truly believe that a revival is coming and that God desires to do amazing, unexplainable, and miraculous stuff. I believe God desires to use your life, your story, and your mouth to speak His words because you did not receive a junior Holy Spirit—you have access to His fullness!

One of the most powerful lines in this entire portion of Scripture is "'For who has understood the mind of the Lord so as to instruct him?' But we have the mind of Christ" (1 Cor. 2:16). Through the indwelling Spirit of Christ and His steering, we can have the mind of Christ. We can be used by Him as if He were here! We as individuals and the church need to once again become little Christs who live in the fullness of the Spirit's power so we, too, can really live as having the mind of Christ!

Giants in the faith like Jonathan Edwards, D.L. Moody, A.B. Simpson, and Billy Graham did not see their ministries grow or fruit produced until they surrendered to the Spirit and allowed Him to do His work. Surrendering to the Spirit's power can do the same for us!

Tozer once said of the church, "If the Holy Spirit was withdrawn from the church today, 95 percent of what we do would go on and no one would know the difference. If the Holy Spirit had been withdrawn from the New Testament church, 95 percent of what they did would stop, and everybody would know the difference."[9] In order to really allow your life to move in the direction it is supposed to, you and I have to let the Spirit take the helm.

---

8 Tozer, *Tozer*, 45.
9 A.W. Tozer, *How to Be Filled with the Holy Spirit* (Chicago: Moody Publishing, 2016), 27.

If you are still struggling with the "how" of surrender, just read the words of the Psalmist in Psalm 46:

> God is our refuge and strength, a very present help in trouble. Therefore we will not fear though the earth gives way, though the mountains be moved into the heart of the sea, though its waters roar and foam, though the mountains tremble at its swelling. *Selah.* There is a river whose streams make glad the city of God, the holy habitation of the Most High. God is in the midst of her; she shall not be moved; God will help her when morning dawns. The nations rage, the kingdoms totter; he utters his voice, the earth melts. The Lord of hosts is with us; the God of Jacob is our fortress. *Selah.* Come, behold the works of the Lord, how he has brought desolations on the earth. He makes wars cease to the end of the earth; he breaks the bow and shatters the spear; he burns the chariots with fire. "Be still and know that I am God. I will be exalted among the nations, I will be exalted in the earth!" The Lord of hosts is with us; the God of Jacob is our fortress. *Selah.*

KEY TAKEAWAY PRINCIPLES

- Allow the Spirit to be at the helm of your ship.
- Understand from where you get your heading (God the Father).
- Do not be afraid to let go of control of your ship/life.
- Release fear and let Him guide your steps.

FURTHER STUDY

- "Jesus said to him, 'I am the way, and the truth, and the life. No one comes to the Father except through me'" (John 14:6).
- "Your word is a lamp to my feet and a light to my path" (Psalm 119:105).
- "You make known to me the path of life; in your presence there is fullness of joy; at your right hand are pleasures forevermore" (Psalm 16:11).

CHAPTER 5
ANCHOR

In our busy society, we often hastily associate connotations to almost every word. For example, green equals go; red equals stop; profits are positive, etc. At first, "anchor" is usually associated with the word *stop*. Sail is positive; anchor is negative. However, every sailor knows the importance of an anchor when you are not moving. It is a stabilizing tool to protect the ship.

On a positive note, the anchor is usually associated with stability, security, and peace of mind. It is easier to sleep at night when you are at anchor when you have confidence that the anchor will not let your ship drift.

There are a few standard components of an anchor. The top loop where you attach the chain is called the eye. The main shaft down the middle is called the shank. The bottom point is called the crown. The two sides that curve upward are called the flukes. Right below the eye on the shank is a cross post called the stock. Where the stock and shank intersect, it looks like a cross. Therefore, Christian generations used the anchor as a symbol of salvation and hope.

Once at anchor, there are some usual characteristics that are known and must be observed. The ship will almost always point into the wind while at anchor. The hull of the ship has an aerodynamic shape, most notably the pointed bow. The wind and current will flow around that shape. When the wind changes, all the ships at anchorage in the same bay will move together. If the anchorage is deep and more anchor chain is needed, this may mean the ship will have a farther distance from the anchor and may drift farther in varying wind patterns.

Sea anchors are not very common with big ships anymore. Sea anchors (and drogues) are still used today and often look similar to an underwater parachute. But in the past, a sea anchor was very important in a storm. The purpose of a sea anchor was to stabilize the ship from drifting too fast. During a storm, you do not want the wind pushing you in the wrong direction. The sea anchor slows down the ship till the storm is over or control can be regained. In today's world, we see the storms of life and do not know how to lay anchor. The Bible is full of ways in which we can anchor ourselves properly in the stormy times of life. Let us take a peek at four such anchors.

It is no secret that we have been living in stormy times. We have recently seen a lingering pandemic, joblessness, riots, and unnecessary deaths. We have seen seen many lose loved ones, and we have seen the pain of severe accidents. Yet the Bible offers us the hope of certainty in the middle of uncertain times. Tozer once said, "God is the God of today and tomorrow as well as yesterday. However, to most Christians, God is the God of yesterday alone. They believe in everything that was but cannot rise to believe for today, let alone tomorrow."[10]

It is easy to believe the promises for those in the past. We have seen His faithfulness. But now? Certainty during these stormy times? Really? Yes, we truly can put our trust in the promises of the Lord.

As believers, we have the promises of God on which to lean. We can cling to the Scriptures. We have the example of the early church and Christ Himself to imitate. Yet we doubt. We allow the uncertainty to bog us down, to cloud our memories, and to cause us to stumble in believing the promises of God. The question we must ask, then, is how can we find certainty in stormy times?

STUDY FIRST

Read Isaiah 53:4-5; Psalm 23; Matthew 8:14-17; 1 Peter 2:18-25.

---

[10] A. W. Tozer and James L. Snyder, *A Cloud by Day, A Fire by Night: Finding and Following God's Will for You* (Minneapolis: Bethany House Publishers, 2019), 121.

Let us look at four anchors we can hoist over our ship to keep us secure in stormy times.

ANCHOR #1: FOLLOWING THE FOOTSTEPS OF CHRIST ALWAYS LEADS TO CERTAINTY

To say the early church lived in the thick of uncertainty would be an understatement. These early Christians did not have the certainty of tomorrow. Every time they gathered, they could be arrested. Every time they declared their allegiance to Christ, they could be martyred. Every baptism could be a government setup. They could live or die tomorrow. Yet Peter offers hope and certainty. Those circumstances were true, but they were called to this. Peter reminds them that following Jesus brought with it the promise of difficulty and uncertainty.

As believers, Peter reminds us of our call to be willing to suffer for the sake of the Kingdom. Karen Jobes says, "Peter's call is to suffer unjustly, to suffer even though one has done nothing to provoke or deserve it, simply because one is a Christian. The challenge of the call doesn't stop there; Peter further exhorts the Christian to keep on doing good even when unjustly suffering."[11] This call is hard, yet we have a great example in Christ on how to do it!

Christ left us a color-by-number painting to find certainty in uncertain times—Himself! I love this imagery. Edmund Clowney said, "The word Peter used for 'example' could also apply to an artist's sketch to be filled in, or another way to think of it—a color by number painting."[12] The Greek word *hypogrammos* means "model, pattern to be copied in writing or drawing."[13] Wow! We have the sketch of certainty. We must follow it.

How often, though, do we try to draw our own painting of certainty? I am terrible at painting. Without a paint-by-numbers direction, I would create

---

[11] Karen H. Jobes, *Baker Exegetical Commentary on the New Testament: 1 Peter*, vol. 21 (Grand Rapids: Baker Academic, 2005), 192.
[12] Edmund P. Clowney, *Bible Speaks Today: 1 Peter,* vol. 18 (Westmont: InterVarsity Press, 1988), 118.
[13] Ibid.

something awful. Jesus left an example of humility, meekness, and kindness in the middle of uncertainty. He did not react to the uncertainty. He rested peacefully within it. We can be like Christ because we have the Holy Spirit!

The believer can follow Christ's footsteps only through submission to the Holy Spirit. The Spirit is the One Who illuminates the numbers on the painting. He alone empowers us to paint the proper picture.

ANCHOR #2: LEAVING EVERYTHING IN THE HANDS OF THE LORD LEADS TO CERTAINTY

In my humanness, I like control. I want to be in control as much as I possibly can. We see this in the life of Peter, too. In the gospels, we see Peter repeatedly trying to gain control of the situation. He gets shot down by Jesus every time. Jesus rebukes him harshly. Yet as Peter watched Jesus and saw His example, he saw the God-Man entrust everything over to the Lord. Jesus, Who had every right to gain control, entrusted everything to His Father! Peter states, "[He] continued entrusting himself to him who judges justly" (1 Peter 2:23).

Jesus did not need to try and control His uncertainty. While He was being beaten, whipped, slapped, falsely accused, and His disciples scattered, Jesus entrusted Himself to the Father. He knew and believed the promises of God and entrusted Himself to those promises.

Norman Hillyer reminds us, "Believers are not left to face suffering solely in their own strength, which might well prove inadequate."[14] I would say we are completely inadequate and should seek to walk in suffering and uncertainty, leaning on and entrusting fully in the Judge Who judges justly. Hillyer continues, "But it is noteworthy that Peter uses the present tense: God, he says, judges justly. At all times and in every situation, God's discernment is perfect and his verdict just and true."[15]

In the middle of uncertainty, God is in control. His judgment is always perfect. We may not know *why* certain things have played out the way they

---

14 Norman Hillyer, *1 and 2 Peter, Jude* (Grand Rapids: Baker Books, 2011), 85.
15 Ibid.

have, but we can entrust ourselves to the Lord. We can always learn from Him in adversity. Tozer says, "As we give ourselves to the Lord and trust Him through the bad times, we finally come to see that what God was doing was something we never imagined."[16] I love this because God is always on the move. We must simply trust Him in all times, not just the good. We must stop striving for control and simply give up control.

ANCHOR #3: THE WOUNDS OF CHRIST HEAL ALL WOUNDS AND BRING CERTAINTY TO LIFE

Christ *died* for us. This is a certainty for us as believers. No matter what, our hope is anchored in the cross. His wounds empower our holiness. His wounds break apart the power of Satan, sin, and death. His wounds enable us to stand strong in the midst of adversity or uncertainty. The certainty of the cross breaks the power of uncertainty in our lives.

There is no need to fear because of His wounds. There is no need to be anxious about tomorrow because of His wounds. His atonement rights all wrongs. When we truly believe in Him, these are truths to which we cling. We must allow His wounds to guide and direct our certainty. Peter needed to remind the early church and us of this certainty.

Christ was wounded so we did not need to be. Here, the Lord promises suffering, but he also promises healing. Christ died so that we could be empowered by the Spirit to do His will, to live righteously, and to die to sin. It is only through the cross that this is possible. Tozer once said, "When God leads us to do something for Him, He always empowers us to do it."[17] It is the atonement that empowers us to do the something God is calling us to do.

One of the greatest truths of the atoning sacrifice of Christ is that there is healing in the atonement! We must also see the promise of deep inner healing as well as physical healing in these passages. Simpson stated, "This phrasing in Isaiah and Peter must mean physical redemption through His

---

16 Tozer, *A Cloud*.
17 Tozer, *A Cloud*, 122.

agony as our substitute."[18] Part of the Christian and Missionary Alliance's Fourfold Gospel is "Christ our Healer." These verses have a history in our denomination proving this fact. Coupling the three books makes this a solid foundational truth. Jesus heals us spiritually, emotionally, and physically. He took all our infirmities. We may not always receive the healing we want, but we will always get the healing we need. Healing is promised in the atonement.

ANCHOR #4: CERTAINTY IS FOUND IN RETURNING TO THE SHEPHERD

I have said it before, and I will say it again: sheep are dumb—plain and simple. They wander. They easily get lost. They are constantly trying to kill themselves, and they need the shepherd to snatch them out of the jaws of death. A wandering sheep has no certainty of safety. A wandering sheep has no direction.

Only in the presence of our true Shepherd can we truly have certainty. He is there. His voice is speaking. He is active, even when it does not seem like it. He is working all things together for our good (Rom. 8:28).

The Lord's presence is the only place to find certainty in an uncertain world (Psalm 23). Only with the Shepherd can we find comfort, safety, discipline, and rest. Only in the presence of the Shepherd can we lie down and live free of the fear of evil. Not only is Peter soliciting more thoughts on Isaiah 53 here but also on Psalm 23. Wandering from the Shepherd's care and oversight of our lives leads to uncertainty that overwhelms us and brings fear. Within the sheepfold in the Shepherd's presence is where we find true rest.

May we decide today to return to our Shepherd, find healing in the wounds of Christ, entrust everything we have to Him, and follow in the footsteps of Christ. Only then can we find the certainty our souls desperately desire in such an uncertain world.

---

18 A.B. Simpson, *Days of Heaven Upon Earth* (Harrisburg: Christian Publishers, 1897), 129.

KEY TAKEAWAY PRINCIPLES

- The anchor is associated with stability, security, and peace of mind.
- The anchor is a stabilizing force.
- The anchor is a hidden symbol of the cross of salvation and hope.

FURTHER STUDY

- "Now when the south wind blew gently, supposing that they had obtained their purpose, they weighed anchor and sailed along Crete, close to the shore" (Acts 27:13).
- "After hoisting it up, they used supports to undergird the ship. Then, fearing that they would run aground on the Syrtis, they lowered the gear,[a] and thus they were driven along" (Acts 27:17).
- "We have this as a sure and steadfast anchor of the soul, a hope that enters into the inner place behind the curtain" (Heb. 6:19).

CHAPTER 6
RIGGING

The sails usually get the credit for moving the ship, but the rigging is essential in the process. Ropes are attached to the key components of the ship. They tie the ship to the dock when they are at port. Ropes (eventually chains) were tied to the anchors. They are attached to the sails. They can even be used as handrails, protective railings, and to hang a hammock for the crew members. It was also common to have ropes in the crow's nest. Even during a storm, there had to be a lookout. This was an extremely dangerous duty, and the pitching of the ship could actually toss a lookout off the mast. For safety, the crew might tie themselves to the mast or to the crow's nest.

The phrase "run a tight ship" usually refers to taut ropes. This saying usually refers to making sure everything is shipshape. Running a tight ship means having a well-organized, disciplined ship and crew.

Ask a Christian what the "rigging" of the Christian faith is and you will generally find five different answers. The first says the rigging is right doctrine. If you have the utmost correct doctrine possible, you are solid as a Christian. Yet Jesus says the demons have correct doctrine but are demons still! Other Christians might say it is all about correct behavior. If one acts morally, is kind, goes to church, tithes, votes the moral party, obeys their parents, and reads the Bible often, they are rigged properly. Jesus saw the Pharisees and noted their great morality and their powerful knowledge of the Bible. Yet they were "full of dead people's bones" (Matt. 23:27).

Still other Christians will say your rigging is in correct ministry. If you are ministering somewhere, you are rigged well to the ship of your life. Yet many have found as they have entered ministry, they lose their soul, and the ship of their life goes down in flames. Other believers would say it is all about the right experiences. If you go on missions trips and see healings and miracles and crazy, wild "God stuff" happen, then your rigging is strong!

I believe that the proper rigging of the soul is correct relationship. You see, if we are in correct relationship with the Lord, then we will have a proper view of Who He is (doctrine); we will have a deep desire to please Him with our whole lives (behavior); we will walk as He walked on the earth, serving Him wherever He calls (ministry); and finally, we will experience the fullness of the truth of His promises (experience).[19]

Rigging of the soul boils down to the relational connection we have to the Source of life. Dallas Willard describes this connection as "the intentional and continuous ordering of one's orientation toward *living all of life in the Spirit*. Christian spirituality necessitates a *willing surrender* to the reigning presence of Christ. It is more a relational process than a list of dos and don'ts. You surrender to Jesus as King over *everything*—thoughts, words, deeds" [emphasis mine].[20]

The rigging of our lives is based on a relational connection to Jesus through the Holy Spirit. So, if our rigging is more of a relational process, how do we cultivate that relationship? I believe, as Richard Foster does, it is through the spiritual disciplines.

To really give an accurate picture of "good rigging," I want to follow the layout of Foster from his book *List of Spiritual Disciplines* to better help you

---

19 Dr. Ron Walborn, "Session 1: The Garden Concept," Advanced Theological Seminary, May 27, 2016,YouTube video, 21:38, https://www.youtube.com/watch?v=TwFqaqkaUYw&list=PL34iKQ5Nu0v1RDqTdgB1-lxlB7V7nX4qO&index=2.
20 Dallas Willard, *The Spirit of the Disciplines: Understanding How God Changes Lives* (San Francisco: HarperSanFrancisco, 1999), 56.

develop your own "strong rigging." Let us start with what he calls the "inward disciplines" of meditation, prayer, fasting, and study/journaling.

MEDITATION

Meditation is first and foremost a slowing down from and a silencing of the chaos and noise around us. It is a lingering focus on God's Word and a purposeful listening to the Lord's voice. Meditation is important for *knowing* the Lord, as opposed to just knowing *about* Him.[21] "Christian meditation, very simply, is the ability to hear God's voice and obey it."[22]

PRAYER

Prayer is communicating with God and making space for Him to communicate with you. Honesty in prayer is essential. "Prayer will increase in power and reality as we repudiate all pretense and learn to be utterly honest before God as well as before men."[23]

Prayer is essential in our lives because it is our primary connection to the Lord's personal voice to us and our honest words to Him.[24]

FASTING

"Throughout Scripture fasting refers to abstaining from food for spiritual purposes."[25] Today, I believe it can be fasting from other things we see as a "primary sustainer." Generally, fasting is a personal discipline but can be a corporate one as well.

Fasting must center on God, and it reminds us Who sustains us. It is not food (or other seeming sustainers). Fasting can bring breakthroughs in the

---

21 Genesis 24:63; Psalm 1:2; Psalm 63:6; Psalm 119:148; 1 Samuel 3:1-8; 1 Kings 19:9-18; Matthew 14:13.
22 Richard Foster and Kathryn A. Helmers, *Celebration of Discipline: The Path to Spiritual Growth* (London: Hodder, 2008), 17.
23 A. W. Tozer and Warren W. Wiersbe, *The Best of A.W. Tozer* (Camp Hill: WingSpread Publishers, 2007), 44.
24 Psalms 118:5-6; Psalm 138:3; Isaiah 58:9-11; Matthew 6:5-13; Philippians 4:6-7; 1 Peter 5:7.
25 Richard Foster and Kathryn A. Helmers, *Celebration of Discipline: The Path to Spiritual Growth* (London: Hodder, 2008), 48.

spiritual realm that will never happen in any other way. There is an element of sacrifice here as well—one we declare we are willing to make in order to experience a deepening of our relationship with Christ.[26] [27]

STUDY/JOURNALING

Taking time to study the whole Word, or small portions of it, is key to spiritual growth. It is not everyone's primary way of connecting but one we must undertake to *know* more of God. Journaling helps assist in recalling what we have learned and what God has done in, through, and for us. My advice to all believers who want to strengthen their rigging is to study widely and study deeply. Read devotionals or theologically challenging books by authors to whom you may not normally gravitate. Do not always seek out the voices with whom you know you will agree. Be challenged. One thing many believers often do is live in a Christian bubble that only serves as an echo chamber. Allow those who are biblically sound but may have a different view to strengthen your rigging.[28]

Now that we have looked at the "inner disciplines," let us study what Foster calls the "outward disciplines" of simplicity, solitude, submission, and service.

SIMPLICITY

"The Christian discipline of simplicity is an *inward* reality that results in an *outward* lifestyle. Both the inward and the outward aspects of simplicity are essential."[29] We choose inwardly to live off less. We make a conscience decision to decomplicate life. This then affects our outward lifestyle. Simplicity is being content with little and is "the joy of possessing nothing!"[30] Seeking the

---

[26] Ezra 8:23; Judges 20:26; 1 Samuel 7:6, 31:13; 2 Chronicles 20:3-4; 1 Kings 21:27-29; Isaiah 58:3-7; Matthew 4:1-11; Luke 2:37.
[27] Here is a great resource for fasting, which utilizes these Scriptures: https://www.thenivbible.com/blog/10-biblical-purposes-fasting.
[28] The Psalms and Lamentations
[29] Foster, ibid, 79.
[30] A.W. Tozer, *The Pursuit of God* (Abbotsford: Aneko Press, updated 2015).

Kingdom of God first and foremost for Who He is rather than what He gives is vital for this discipline to flourish. This is hard in a consumeristic society but is very healthy for the believer because it serves to declutter their life.[31]

SOLITUDE

"Settle yourself in solitude, and you will come upon Him in yourself."[32] God longs to be with us, *just* us. Solitude is more of a state of mind than a specific place, but specific places can lead us better into solitude. A good tool of centering prayer is this helpful phrase mentioned by Brennan Manning: "Abba, I belong to you."[33] As you are alone, breathe this in and out. It is helpful to get quiet in the middle of your solitude. Meditation happens best in solitude.[34]

SUBMISSION

"In submission we are at last free to value other people."[35] When we surrender all, we have all to gain. Bending our knee to the will of the One Who loves us best is medicine for the soul. Submission stops us from wasting time on our agenda, which will not work. Following His agenda does work. Submission also helps us make others more important than ourselves and love our neighbor as ourselves because we are submitting to His Word, which calls us to do such things.[36]

SERVICE

Bernard of Clairvaux is known for saying, "Learn the lesson that, if you are to do the work of a prophet, what you need is not the scepter (to rule) but a hoe

---

31 James 1:10-11; 2:5-6; Luke 12:13-21; 16:10-12; Matthew 6:25-34.
32 "Saint Teresa Of Avila Quote – Settle Yourself In Solitude . . . " Onejourney.Net, Accessed November 1, 2022, Https://Onejourney.net/Saint-Teresa-Of-Avila-Quote-Settle-Yourself-In-Solitude.
33 Brennan Manning, *The Furious Longing of God* (Colorado Springs, CO: David C. Cook, 2009), 46 and 58.
34 Biblical Basis: Psalm 46:10; Lamentations 3:25-28; Exodus 33:7-11; 1 Kings 19; Luke 5:16; Mark 1:35; Matthew 14:13.
35 Richard Foster and Kathryn A. Helmers, *Celebration of Discipline: The Path to Spiritual Growth* (London: Hodder, 2008), 112.
36 James 4:7; 1 Peter 5:5; Romans 8:28-29; Matthew 10:39; Galatians 2:20; 5:25.

(to serve)." Another way of saying this would be, "Rule with the heart of a servant and serve with the heart of the King." True service is seeking to wash the feet of your brother or sister in Christ. Jesus displayed this type of loving service well in the book of John when He stooped down to wash the dirty feet of His disciples. We, too, are called to get dirty, get low, and serve others. We do not live on this earth to live for and serve ourselves, but as believers, we live to serve others.[37]

Finally, Foster discusses what he calls "corporate disciplines"—confession, worship, and celebration.

CONFESSION

St. Augustine, a prominent leader in the early church, stated, "The confession of evil works is the first beginning of good works."[38] In essence, without confession, our works are tainted. Confession to the Lord allows us to be forgiven. Confession to our brothers and sisters allows us to see forgiveness. When darkness comes into light, it loses its power. Confession is bringing to light the things we like to hide in the darkness.

The enemy is known as the prince of darkness, and when we walk in darkness, we are walking in and choosing the territory of the enemy. Confession is not to just be done to the Lord but also to one another so we can encourage one another to "walk in the light, as he is in the light" (1 John 1:7). We call this corporate because we are not just alone with the Lord in this, but we should be confessing to one another.[39]

WORSHIP

William Temple once declared, "To worship is to quicken the conscience by the holiness of God, to feed the mind with the truth of God, to purge

---

37 Proverbs 11:25; Matthew 23:11; Mark 10:45; Romans 12:9-13; Galatians 6:10; Acts 20:35; Colossians 3:23-24; Matthew 25:40; John 13:1-17.
38 "Augusta of Hippo›Quotes›Quotable Quote," Goodreads.com, Accessed October 16, 2022, https://www.goodreads.com/quotes/721218-the-confession-of-evil-works-is-the-first-beginning-of.
39 1 John 1:9-10; James 5:16; Psalm 32:3-5; Ephesians 4:25; 5:8-9; Proverbs 28:13; Psalm 130.

the imagination by the beauty of God, to open the heart to the love of God, to devote the will to the purpose of God."[40] Worship is in everything we do and say, not just the songs we sing. He is the object of our worship. If we do not worship Him, we will worship something or someone. We were created to worship, and worship we will. Our modern concept of worship is singing and praising God through music, but it is so much more than that. Whatever we do, whether it is work or play, we should be worshipping Him together and privately.[41]

CELEBRATION

When we gather as the body of believers, we celebrate all the good things the Lord has done. I always liken this to the huge celebration that happens at the end of Nehemiah. God had promised Nehemiah he would be used to rebuild the wall. Through the hammer and sword and filled with God's power and providence, the wall was built. Once it was built, all of Israel came out to have a huge party in celebration of what God had done! When God shows up in our lives or in the life of our church, we need to throw a party and celebrate together! The gathering of believers (not just in the confines of the church building) is a time to worship through song, hearing of the Word, and fellowship.[42]

Adding these areas of rigging to your soul will go a long way to strengthen the ties you have to your Anchor, Jesus Christ. Never neglect the full weight of importance upon relational intimacy with the Lord. Your connection to Him is truly all that matters, and you need a strong rigging to hold you fast.

---

40 "William Temple›Quotes›Quotable Quote," Goodreads.com, Accessed October 27, 2022, https://www.goodreads.com/quotes/441116-to-worship-is-to-quicken-the-conscience-by-the-holiness.
41 Genesis 4:4-5; Hebrews 12:18; 1 Corinthians 10:31, 14:25; Romans 1:25; Acts 16:14.
42 Nehemiah 12; 13:1-3; 1 Corinthians 10:31; Colossians 3:23; Proverbs 17:22.

KEY TAKEAWAY PRINCIPLES

- Don't trip over an unsecured line.
- Don't be dragged in the wrong direction—tie yourself down if necessary.
- Run a tight ship.

FURTHER STUDY

- "We have this as a sure and steadfast anchor of the soul, a hope that enters into the inner place behind the curtain" (Heb. 6:19).
- "Your cords hang loose; they cannot hold the mast firm in its place or keep the sail spread out. Then prey and spoil in abundance will be divided; even the lame will take the prey" (Isa. 33:23).

CHAPTER 7
CROW'S NEST

The crow's nest is the highest point on the ship and provides the best vantage point for scouting the horizon. The crow's nest is a platform that is attached around the main mast of the ship. The lookouts would keep a sharp eye out for any hazards, such as other ships, reefs, storms, and even icebergs. It was the best observational device until the invention of the radar.

Symbolically, the crow's nest is a positive image that helps to determine future dangers. A nest is a home for birds. Climbing the ladders to this position on a pitching ship can be a little difficult for the faint of heart. But once you make it to the nest, you have a sigh of relief. In Greek mythology, crows were considered a symbol of prophecy—thus connected with the future. In some cultures, crows were a symbol of mysteries or magical events in life.

Often, the future adventure that awaits on the other side of the horizon will be full of mysteries and challenges. Vision and sight are extremely important concepts in the Bible. Keep your eyes and heart open to God's message.

Without someone in the crow's nest, the entire ship can get surprised by pirates or a violent storm. If the lookout in the nest is not vigilant and awake enough to be aware of the oncoming issue, the entire ship of men and women suffers. The Scriptures are replete with warnings to "stay awake," "pay attention,"[43] "keep watch!"[44] or phrases quite similar to these. If this is a constant warning, should we not also keep watch over our souls or, as we have been likening them to, our ships? The answer is simple: yes!

---

43 Ephesians 5:14; Luke 21:36; Matthew 24:42; 1 Peter 1:13; Revelation 16:15.
44 Matthew 24:42-44; Matthew 25:13; Exodus 12:42; Habakkuk 2:1; Proverbs 16:17; 1 Timothy 4:16.

I believe King David gives us some great examples of how we can do just that. In Psalm 139:23-24, we see the psalmist cry out, "Search me, O God, and know my heart! Try me and know my thoughts! And see if there be any grievous way in me, and lead me in the way everlasting!"

This is the cry of the lookout. He is asking the Lord to show him the areas he may not be seeing. He is seeking the Lord's vision to see the icebergs in his life or the oncoming storm or the enemy who would seek to derail his life by invading his ship. The Lord loves to answer this question, but we have got to be prepared to hear what the Lord says!

The Holy Spirit of God may point to areas of your heart with which you need to deal. Remember what Peter says: "So put away all malice and all deceit and hypocrisy and envy and all slander. Like newborn infants, long for the pure spiritual milk, that by it you may grow up into salvation" (1 Peter 2:1-2). Those areas of sin *will* be pointed out by the Holy Spirit. When He does, we need to release them, surrender in obedience, and lay those things down.

I once had a dream from the Lord that did this very thing. In my dream, I was a rancher (ha, fat chance in reality!), and I had cattle—in particular, a *huge* red and black bull. This bull was my prized possession in the dream. I fed the bull, loved the bull, and allowed the bull to graze. Yet one day, the bull began to be ornery. He even began to chase my wife and kids. Even after this, I continued to allow the bull to have a huge part of my time. One day, the bull got out and was chasing down my family. I knew that if I did not do something, the bull would kill them all. I had a choice: kill the bull or let it kill my family. I knew what I had to do, so I wished for a gun because after all, guns can magically appear in your hands in dreams. The gun appeared; I took aim; and I shot the bull I loved so much.

Before I woke up, the dream changed and focused in on a woman's backside. She was wearing skintight black jeans, and she had a bright red rear pocket. I immediately woke up and heard the Lord interpret the dream for me. The bull was my lust and pornographic addiction as symbolized by the woman's backside. If I did not handle this bull and seek its death, eventually, the bull would murder my future family. I remember that dream like it was yesterday because it was the day I put a stake in the ground against the lustful bull in my life, and I have been keeping a watch ever since to make sure that bull stays clear of my ship.

We have got to be the watchmen over our hearts. We must maintain our position in the crow's nest. One very important mentor of mine, Dr. Ron Walborn, gave me some good advice on this issue. He gave me this set of questions I should regularly ask myself about my connection to the Lord and what makes me desire more of Him:

- "What are the habits that nourish the life of God within me?
- Who are the people who nourish the life of God within me?
- Where are the places that nourish the life of God within me?"

He then said, "Whatever the answers are, run *to* these habits, people, and places!"

Then, there are these questions about my disconnection to the Lord and what causes me to ignore God or stop desiring Him:

- "What are the habits that choke off the life of God within me?
- Who are the people who choke off the life of God within me?
- Where are the places that choke off the life of God within me?"

He then said, "Whatever the answers are, run *from* these habits, people, and places."

In order for us to maintain the heading of our life, we have to keep a close eye on the horizon and ensure there will be no obstacles that will get in our way that can take down the ship. Sometimes, running to the right things and from the wrong things can be tough, but if we are connected to the Lord, the running to and the running from become a whole lot easier.

KEY TAKEAWAY PRINCIPLES

- Keep focused on the horizon—stay connected to God's vision for your life.
- Keep an eye out for trouble—pray that God would show you trouble ahead, like he did for David.
- If in doubt, take the high ground (if on land). At sea, take refuge in a safe harbor.

FURTHER STUDY

- "The hearing ear and the seeing eye, the Lord has made them both" (Prov. 20:12).
- "Now faith is the assurance of things hoped for, the conviction of things not seen" (Heb. 11:1).
- "'He has blinded their eyes and hardened their heart, lest they see with their eyes, and understand with their heart, and turn, and I would heal them'" (John 12:40).
- "The eyes of the Lord are in every place, keeping watch on the evil and the good" (Prov. 15:3).

CHAPTER 8
GANGWAY

The gangway is used to board and disembark a ship. It is usually a ramp with handrails on both sides. If it is a military ship, it is usually customary to salute the flag (located at the stern of the ship) as you board. The security check is usually located at the end of the gangway. This is the essential location to check the identity, credentials, and purpose of the person boarding the ship. The gangway is sometimes compared to other entry locations, such as gates and doors.

Many biblical heroes started off well. Many of them walked in faith and obedience early on. Many were used for mighty works and achieved great things! King Saul was one who started off well but ended in disaster. His successor, King David, fared much better. King David's life gives us several things we can add to our lives to start and end well. I see the gangway as "the end of the road," where we are disembarking from the voyage. It could be the end of a job, a season, or life. I will then have us look through the lens of living in such a way that we can end well.

Early in my ministry career, I had a boss who, at first, was incredible to work for; but as time went on, he became an oppressive leader over me. My wife can attest that it was some of the darkest days in my life. One example of the struggle was when he asked me to preach one Sunday. I reminded him that he had said I could be gone that weekend and that I would only be getting back Saturday night. I said that I would be happy to preach but asked if it could be moved to another weekend, since he was still going to be in town. He then lashed out at me in full force, screaming and demanding I did as he said because it was his pulpit and his church. How dare I try to subvert his authority by asking for another time to preach, he said. He cussed me out and screamed. Needless to say, it was ugly. Many such tactics were used from that time on. I went home and cried. Then, a wonderful mentor of mine told me to study David's life, and I would eventually find out why he was sending me there.

The enemy was beating me up in ministry, and there were times when I just wanted to quit, walk away from the church, and walk away from God for a time. But this story of how David responded to the attacks of the enemy kept me going because God was with David. His son Absalom was not listening to God, but David was. We have times when we want to give up or even give in to the enemy and his lies, but I think David's life gives us some insight on how to end well. How can we respond well when the enemy is attacking?

STUDY FIRST

Read 2 Samuel 15-19.

David is known as "the man after God's own heart," and the story of Absalom gives us just one glimpse of why. If you and I are going to end well, we need to follow David's example and have a commitment to God that rises above everything else. His life displays well the necessary ingredients for ending well and staying off the gangplank. In his life, we see total trust in God, a faithfulness to God's ways, and a patient heart that waited on the Lord. We, too, need to add these ingredients to our own lives.

TOTAL TRUST IN GOD

Absalom was acting out of self-ambition, seeking his own good. He was lying about his father and turning the hearts of the men around him toward himself, not toward David—and certainly not toward God. Absalom's goal was to be king and the ruler of Israel, and he did not care if he divided the kingdom or not. His trust was in himself and his own abilities. Absalom was even willing to use God's name to get his way with his father (2 Sam. 15:7-9). David, however, had total trust in God.

In his book *A Tale of Three Kings,* Gene Edwards writes about Saul, David, and Absalom and powerfully describes David's thought process. It is an expanded tale, and it reads like a play. Here is an excerpt about this portion of the story:

> "You were not an Absalom, and you refuse to be a Saul. Sir, if you are not willing to put Absalom down, then I suggest we prepare to evacuate the kingdom. For Absalom will surely take the throne." "Only as surely as King Saul killed the shepherd boy," replied the wise old king. "What?" asked Abishai, startled. "Think on it, Abishai. God once delivered a defenseless shepherd boy from the powerful, mad king. He can yet deliver an old ruler from an ambitious young rebel." "You underestimate your adversary," retorted Abishai. "You underestimate my God," replied David serenely."[45]

One of the enemy's tricks is to get us to focus on the pains and struggles of the "right now," causing us to forget the faithfulness of God in the past. We can get so focused on *now* that we miss what He did *then;* and His track record, when seen through hindsight, is flawless. *If God took care of me then, what would cause Him to neglect to do so now?*

Absalom was not following the Lord, yet David was still seeking the heart of God. David was not seeking his own glory, but God's. He trusted God and could do so because he reflected on the goodness of God up to that point.

REMAIN FAITHFUL TO GOD'S WAYS (2 SAM. 16:11-13)

Here, David is being mocked by someone long forgotten. His men want to show this dude what-for, but David remains faithful to God's way. The

---

[45] Gene Edwards, *Tale of Three Kings: A Study in Brokenness* (Wheaton: Tyndale House Publishers, 1992), 76.

Word of God was written on David's heart, and he knew the truth of these words long before his son Solomon would write these words: "Do not say, 'I will repay evil'; wait for the LORD, and he will deliver you" (Prov. 20:22). Peter said something similar in the New Testament: "Do not repay evil for evil or reviling for reviling, but on the contrary, bless, for to this you were called, that you may obtain a blessing" (1 Peter 3:9).

David knew he did not need to repay this evil and that God would either bless him or deliver him. This may be one of the most challenging ways to respond well when the enemy is attacking, especially in our culture. We do not want to respond God's way. We desire to respond our way. We want vengeance. We want those who are persecuting us or hindering us to pay for their interference or persecution. But God's way is different. When we live our lives God's way, we can—and will—end well.

When my boss was screaming his head off at me and causing me to cry, I admit I did not handle it God's way. I began to talk about it widely, even with other staff members. I talked about him behind his back. I sought elders to help me. I talked with my mentors, and I was not about to hold back in my defamation of my boss.

It was then that my mentor, seeing I was on the brink of some destruction, sent me to David's life, as well as the book I mentioned above, *The Tale of Three Kings*. I had to read both of them several times before I would allow the Holy Spirit to soften my heart. God then asked me to seek forgiveness from my boss, admit what I had done, and ask forgiveness, all while he had not yet apologized to me!

I had to make a hard choice: allow the Spirit to lead me down God's way or to lead myself down the wrong path. Eventually, I listened to the Spirit and went God's way, but it took a *long* time—six months to be exact. Although it is not easy, it is best for us during attacks, hard times, and persecution to continue following God's ways. The only way is to trust God and rely on His Spirit.

WAIT ON GOD (2 SAM. 19:12-15)

Here, we see David is not taking the kingdom back by force. Absalom is dead, and the kingdom is rightfully David's, yet he waits. If God truly desires him to have the kingdom back, he can wait on God to make it happen. He does not need to force himself back to the throne. God will make a way. Alan Redpath gave a great window into this when he said, "[David's] return to sovereignty was decided by the voluntary submission of his kinsmen and by their loving obedience to his will."[46]

Here we see the utter difference between kings like Absalom and Saul and a king like David. Saul and Absalom used fear to reign and forced people to bow to them. David waits for the bowing to come voluntarily. He does not need to force people to bow to his rule. He rules differently. David trusted that God would move their hearts, and he waited on God.

In the continuing drama in *A Tale of Three Kings*, Edwards describes what was going on with David in this monologue:

> "I will do what I did under Saul. I will leave the destiny of the kingdom in God's hands alone. Perhaps he is finished with me. Perhaps I have sinned too greatly and am no longer worthy to lead. Only God knows if that is true, and it seems he will not tell." Then, clenching his fist, yet with a touch of wry humor in his voice, David added emphatically, "But today I shall give ample space for this untelling God of ours to show us his will. I know of no other way to bring about such an extraordinary event except by doing nothing! The throne is not mine. Not to have, not to take, not to protect, and not to keep."[47]

Many forces will come against us. Many storms will wage war against our lives. Much of who we are is forged in these storms. In fact, many could say it is the storms that help to make the person. It is not the storms themselves but

---

46 Alan Redpath, *The Making of a Man of God: Lessons from the Life of David* (Grand Rapids: Fleming H. Revell, 2004), 266.
47 Gene Edwards, *Tale of Three Kings: A Study in Brokenness* (Wheaton: Tyndale House Publishers, 1992), 97.

how we choose to navigate the storms that defines us. It will prove to be very difficult to wait on God, for God's timing is not man's timing. We will want to rush ahead, but we need to be people who are seeking His voice to know whether it is time or not. Even when the way seems clear to run out and go for it, we still may need to wait a little longer on the Lord.

Be more like David than Absalom. David trusted God, followed God's way even when it was tough, and then waited on God. Absalom did none of these things, nor did he even desire to do so. Ask the Spirit of God to give you the ability to weather the storms of life well. You may not be going through a storm now, but you will again someday. *End well!*

KEY TAKEAWAY PRINCIPLES

- You have to know where to board and where (how) the adventure begins.
- It is good to know where the nearest exit is.
- Security is important.

FURTHER STUDY

- "'Enter by the narrow gate. For the gate is wide and the way is easy that leads to destruction, and those who enter by it are many. For the gate is narrow and the way is hard that leads to life, and those who find it are few'" (Matt. 7:13-14).
- "Behold, I stand at the door and knock. If anyone hears my voice and opens the door, I will come in to him and eat with him, and he with me" (Rev. 3:20).
- "I am the door. If anyone enters by me, he will be saved and will go in and out and find pasture" (John 10:9).
- "'Ask, and it will be given to you; seek, and you will find; knock, and it will be opened to you'" (Matt. 7:7).

- "'It is easier for a camel to go through the eye of a needle than for a rich person to enter the kingdom of God'" (Mark 10:25).
- "And the twelve gates were twelve pearls, each of the gates made of a single pearl, and the street of the city was pure gold, like transparent glass" (Rev. 21:21).
- "And its gates will never be shut by day—and there will be no night there" (Rev. 21:25).

CHAPTER 9
RUDDER

A rudder is a flat, controlling surface that is hinged vertically at the stern of the ship. It is used for steering the ship. The rudder often symbolizes the free flow of life and the choices we have in life. An individual has control of their fate in their own hands and can pick different directions. The rudder is symbolic of the decisions we make and why we make them.

The words I say can sometimes get me in trouble. Maybe you can relate. In the book of James, we see the tongue being equated with the rudder of a ship. James, led by the Spirit, desires for his readers to know that words carry weight and can direct the life (or vessel) of a person. The tongue, although small, plays a very powerful part in a person's life.

The old saying, "Sticks and stones may break my bones, but words will never hurt me!" is a flat-out lie. Bruises heal. Broken bones mend. Yet when someone declares something over your life with a purpose to wound, those wounds last much longer than physical wounds. Even when a physical wound scars over, the mark of the wound is there; but for the most part, the pain is gone. Words are different. The pain lingers, and the wound festers under the scars.

This, among many reasons, is why James seeks to get the reader to fully grasp the weight the tongue brings to bear on the vessel. It is small, but like a rudder, it has a very big part to play on the voyage. What I am trying to convey is that your words matter, and the words spoken over you matter, too. In the book of Luke, we read, "For out of the abundance of the heart his mouth speaks" (Luke 6:45b). That which is in our heart already will be exposed by what we say.

This brings us back to lies. Many of us have had people *speak* lies over us. We have heard people in our lives call us worthless, fat, ugly, expendable, dispensable, unimportant, annoying, spoiled, whiny, terrible, stupid, useless, an accident, illegitimate, etc. We could go on and on pointing out all the lies that have been spoken over us, but the reality is, none of them are true. Yet those words have many times shaped the way we imagine ourselves. Those words have charted the course of our lives to "prove them wrong."

We have seen the power those words have had in our lives and use them as tools to fight off others as well. Also, sadly, many times, we use those words against ourselves and repeat the lies over and over again to the inner parts of our soul. This is why James was so clear—the tongue is course-setting. Words dictate the way the vessel is pointing.

One of the areas of maintenance for the rudder of our vessel is taking back the truth of our identity. We cannot afford thoughts in our heads that the Lord does not have of us as His children. Words that have negatively impacted us must be brought to the Lord. We must ask the Spirit of God to redirect our course by eliminating the lies and speaking truth into our souls. We cannot allow the lies of others and the enemy to control the trajectory of our ship. Only the Lord, His voice, and the truth of whom He says we are to have the right to direct our vessel.

Next, we must choose to speak words of life and not death. What we speak does reveal our hearts. Is your heart full of hatred or love? Lust or life? Retribution or rejoicing? Your words will expose the truth of where your heart truly is. Take stock of the words you say. Really sit and listen to what comes out of your mouth. As parents or teachers, we must be extra cautious with our words. When we speak words over our children, they take them to heart and often use those words (good or bad) and attach them to the very core of who they are! We as parents, teachers, pastors, and mentors truly have a rudder with our words, and it is not always our own vessel we are affecting!

This can start in your thought life. What are you saying to yourself about yourself? What are you saying to yourself about others? These words not yet spoken can also help indicate where you need a course adjustment. Do not just think of this as nice or quaint advice. Take it to heart. Listen to the Word and get your heart on a better heading as you listen to the words that come out of your mouth and into your head.

KEY TAKEAWAY PRINCIPLES

- Research, plan, and pick the right direction.
- Life is not a straight line.
- Adventurers are sometimes off course. That is okay—readjust.

FURTHER STUDY

- "Look at the ships also: though they are so large and are driven by strong winds, they are guided by a very small rudder wherever the will of the pilot directs" (James 3:4).
- "So they cast off the anchors and left them in the sea, at the same time loosening the ropes that tied the rudders. Then hoisting the foresail to the wind they made for the beach" (Acts 27:40).

CHAPTER 10
POSITIVE OUTWARD APPEARANCE

Maintenance is required to make a ship run properly. A poorly kept vessel displays a lack of leadership, work ethic, and pride in your job. The phrase "run a tight ship" usually refers to taut ropes, but it also refers to making sure all the seams in the ship are caulked—thus *tight* refers to "watertight." This saying usually refers to making sure everything is shipshape. Running a tight ship means having a well-organized, disciplined ship and crew who, in turn, care for the ship.

The need for a well-kept vessel is so great that sometimes, people may try to fake it. We may try to feign good maintenance when in reality, we are just putting on a show. *This* is most dangerous. Let us call this "pretending to be shipshape." When the maintenance is not done, this causes loads of trouble for the voyages ahead. I am going to share from the books of Acts what I mean, and I will use "the stage" as a way of describing this "pretending to be shipshape."

It can be easy to pretend we have it all together or think we have arrived somewhere we actually have not. In the story of Ananias and Sapphira, this was a huge driving force—the appearance of something that was not real, or pretending to be shipshape. George MacDonald once said, "Half of the misery in the world comes from trying to look, instead of trying to be, what one is not."[48] I believe the following Scripture draws out and then answers this question: what does freedom from pretend-based living look like?

---

48 George MacDonald and David L. Neuhouser, *George MacDonald: Selections from His Greatest Works* (New York: Victor Books, 1990), 58.

STUDY FIRST
Read Acts 5:1-11.

Pretending to be shipshape is living a life on a stage. Life *off* the stage is a life of freedom. We need to be off the stage as believers, so we can truly allow the vessel to not just look but truly *be* healthy. We can see, then, from Ananias and Sapphira's story that life off the stage frees us from a life of secrecy.

Moments before this story unfolds, there was a generous donation to the church fund by a man named Barnabas. He had just sold one of his fields and given the entire amount to the church. There was excitement among the people, and many praised Barnabas for his generosity; but Barnabas was doing it out of a heart for the Lord. His desire was not praise or accolades. Barnabas was simply giving out of a deep love for God.

This was not the case with the next couple who gave. There was no mandate to give. But when Ananias and Sapphira saw the glory and praise that Barnabas received, they, too, desired to be among "the Christian elite." So, they conspired to sell and give, but they did not give all. Instead, they planned to say the total was all they had received, thus keeping some cash for themselves and receiving praise for their generosity. For the applause it would bring, they spiraled into a life of secrecy, and it cost them their lives. Their only sin was professing to give everything, when they had only given a part. They were under no obligation to give at all!

We tend to desire to *seem* surrendered when we know we are not (1 John 1:8-10). It is pretense; and it can be seen in singing, testimonies, and embellished stories of courageous evangelism or brushing off that everything in our lives is okay. We, too, have been tricked by the enemy to live lives of secrecy. We care more about the image of the ship than we do the actual reality of the vessel's health. We see others lauded for their righteous deeds and relatively sinless lives, so we hide the real struggles we are going through so we, too, can be praised. We may also be living in secrecy so we are not called out on our sin.

SECRECY WRAPS US IN CHAINS OF BONDAGE (1 JOHN 1:8-10)

God's desire is for us to be free, not locked in the shadows with our secret sins and struggles. Maybe we do not act "surrendered" but act as if we are doing okay when in all honesty, we are dying inside. Church can become a stage to fake it rather than be honest. I am tired of fake Christianity, and I am sure you are, too. If we choose to live stage-free lives, we will be free from secrecy because it will be more about our relationship to the Father than our glory in the stage lights! Life off the stage frees us from the *lying* voice of the faux captain (1 John 1: 3-6; Rev. 12:9-10).

Secrecy, darkness, and shadows—those things are the realm of the enemy, not the realm of the Lord. The enemy of our souls *loves* the darkness; so, if he tries to get you and me to follow him there, he wins. With secrecy, he has some hold over a part of our lives, and that brokenness we keep hidden grows and grows.

The enemy in the "play" is the stage director. He loves for us to be on the stage instead of God. He loves to give out false directions on how we can better our performance so we neglect to go to God. Therefore, Peter says, "Why has Satan filled your heart to lie?" (Acts 5:3). Ananias and Sapphira were taking directions from the faux captain and were neglecting to listen to the true Captain, the Director of their life.

For a long time, I was like them and listened to the lies of the stage director. Peter gives us the biggest clue as to who desires for us to stay hidden. Satan is the prince of darkness (Eph. 6:12).

A good friend of mine in college was always the happy, smiling Christian. I remember being jealous of her constant optimism. For years, this façade never wavered—until God intervened, of course. She realized she was being fake in covering up her deep, inner pain with smiles and fake happiness. She believed that this was what people wanted to see from her, so she hid her pain and pretended to be okay. Then she heard these amazing words, "It's okay not to be okay."

She was freed from the performance trap of being the perfect, happy Christian. She realized she did not need to listen to the lies of the stage director. God offered a different, better way. The chains of bondage from trying to look perfect on the stage of her Christian life were broken. We do not have to be bound to the lies of the enemy (John 8:44). He wants to trick you to remain in bondage to your secrecy. He wants you to perform in a play that will, in the end, get lousy reviews.

LIFE OFF THE STAGE FREES US TO ALWAYS WALK IN THE LIGHT (ACTS 5:7-9; 1 JOHN 1:5-10)

Peter was offering Sapphira a chance to step into the Light, yet she remained in the darkness. She claimed the amount he named was, in fact, the amount she and Ananias had received for the sale. I believe Peter hoped she would come clean and walk in the Light. But she did not. Sapphira chose to continue to put on a play rather than step off the stage. We can be free from the darkness, my friends. We do not need to wallow in the dark hollows of our secret sins or our desire to perform well in front of each other. This was not meant to be the state of the Church! Church does not have to be a place of pretenders but should be a place of love and honesty. Judgment should not be a part of the Church or our personal walks with Christ. Love should open the door for confession and repentance so we can be set free from Satan, sin, and death. We can keep choosing death like Ananias and Sapphira or be set free through the beauty of repentance.

We were never meant to be actors putting on a play called the Christian life. Rather, we are called to walk in the Light! First John 1:5-10 assures us that the *only* way to have real fellowship is to walk in the Light. This is why this sin was so serious. Ananias and Sapphira were lying to the Holy Spirit, as well as to His church!

Once a fake "shipshape" spirit gains a toehold in a community, it brings the end of real fellowship (1 John 1:6-7). Have you been putting on a play? Stage-free living is ours to attain from the Holy Spirit. We can be free to always walk in the Light. No more performing, just living and experiencing true fellowship that God desired for us.

LIFE OFF THE STAGE FREES US TO GO ALL IN AND LIVE REAL LIFE (ACTS 5:10-11)

Not only did Ananias and Sapphira not give all they had, they also never gave of themselves. When we put on a play and walk in the darkness, even when offered to step into the Light, we are not giving ourselves completely over to the Lord or His community. Our lives become dry and fake. The performance takes over, and we do not experience real life the way God intended.

God's heart is that you and I go all in. If we give into the stage, when the world looks upon us, they will see actors. They will see Ananias and Sapphira. Then we will lose our influence in this world! Vance Havner snarkily said, "If God dealt with people today as he did in Ananias and Sapphira's day, every church would need a morgue in the basement!"[49]

Sin is serious, and we must deal with it. If we do not turn away from it, repent, and turn toward God, it will hinder us greatly and chain us in bondage. When we are people who allow the Spirit to get us off the stage of our play and begin to go all in to the work of the Kingdom, people begin to sit up and notice. Authenticity is a magnet that draws in people. When we can be authentic about our real issues and still be embraced and loved by our brothers and sisters as well as helped out of our pits, people notice that type of community and desire it for themselves!

Performance and image killed Ananias and Sapphira. It does not have to kill you. Are you tired of performing? Are you frustrated with the acting and

---

[49] "Acts 5 Commentary," Precept Austin online, Updated May 14, 2022, https://www.preceptaustin.org/acts-5-commentary.

the pretense? Is the secrecy getting to you? Are you done with the "image" that you feel you have to keep up?

God wants you to live in freedom, the freedom that gives you the ability to get off the stage. True living only happens when we are free to stop hiding, when we are free to walk in the Light through confession and repentance. True living happens when we are free to say no to the tempting voice of the enemy. His stage directions always lead to death.

You do not have to act anymore. You can make the choice to get off the stage. If the Holy Spirit has been pricking your heart, today is the day. Be honest about your sin and pain. Do not hide anymore. Confess and repent and turn back to God by getting off the stage.

KEY TAKEAWAY PRINCIPLES

- A well-maintained, clean, and professional vessel could display many concepts: battle-ready, discipline, and pride in your ship.
- A positive image reflects a positive connotation on everyone involved.
- A disorganized or poorly kept vessel often displays laziness and a poor attitude.

FURTHER STUDY

- "Show yourself in all respects to be a model of good works, and in your teaching show integrity, dignity, and sound speech that cannot be condemned, so that an opponent may be put to shame, having nothing evil to say about us" (Titus 2:7-8).
- "In the same way, let your light shine before others, so that[they may see your good works and give glory to your Father who is in heaven" (Matt. 5:16).

CHAPTER 11
COMMUNICATION

There are many different ways to communicate on and with a ship. Here is a list of some of the communication methods:
- Signal flags
- Signal light
- Foghorn
- Lighthouse/shore stations
- Bosun's whistle
- PA system
- Radio (VHF)
- Radio beacons
- Morse code/radio telegraphy
- Digital Selective Calling (DSC) automated distress call
- Satcom

We could take time to discuss how you communicate with other sailors in the ships of life, but I think it is most important to develop communication with your Heavenly Father that is healthy and helpful. Let us call this section "The Way of Prayer."

One of my favorite movies of all time is the cult classic *Monty Python and the Search for the Holy Grail*. One scene in particular cracks me up, and it all has to do with communication. In the scene, guards are charged with taking care of the prince and making sure he does not leave his room. The king gives explicit instructions to the guards, which they cannot seem to fully grasp.

When they ask for clarification, they either add detail or subtract detail, much to the frustration of the king.

I always crack up when I see this scene! Good relationship requires good communication. Poor communication can bring about confusion within a relationship or worse—the end of a relationship. Poor listening can hinder our ability to follow through or to know how we are to live.

Prayer is our communicative connection to God. For many, prayer is simply confusing. How are we to pray? For what are we to pray? And how do we connect relationally to God through prayer? These and many other questions arise when it comes to prayer. There are many scripturally suggested ways of prayer, and today, we will seek to answer the question of what some of the ways of prayer are.

STUDY FIRST

Read Romans 8:26-28; Ephesians 6:18;
Philippians 4:6; 1 Timothy 2:1-2.

Each of these passages describes a way we are to approach communicating with the Lord. I will use the acronym **SIT** to help remember them. This stands for **S**upplication, **I**ntercession, and **T**hanksgiving. It is a reminder that to communicate with the Lord, we need to sit and take time for proper communication. The first way of prayer we will look at is supplication.

PRAYERS OF SUPPLICATION ARE SIMPLY HUMBLE REQUESTS (PHIL. 4:6; 1 TIM. 2:12; EPH. 6:18)

God desires to take care of His children. His heart is to give us good gifts, especially the Holy Spirit. Prayers of supplication freely admit our need for His provision. Prayers are requests from a place of humility, not arrogance.

Supplication comes from a recognition of the Lord's capability, but also of His Sovereignty. Believing that God is all-knowing and all-powerful, we can come to Him with requests; but also knowing that He is Sovereign and

His will is ultimately the most important thing, we pray with expectation but without an agenda. Our humble faith knows God can and will do something, but it also submits ultimately to the will of the Father.

Jesus perfectly displayed this type of prayer in the garden before His arrest. His humble request was that the cup of death be taken away, but in the same breath, He breathed the words, "Your will be done" (Matt. 6:10). Tozer says, "What the praying man does is to bring his will into line with the will of God, so God can do what He has all along been willing to do. Thus, prayer changes the man and enables God to change things in answer to man's prayer."[50]

Worry can be expelled by expectant prayer. Many times, we are driven to prayer out of anxiety. We move into supplication for ourselves or others because we are moved with worry. We desire a certain outcome to free us from the worry the issue is causing, so we go to prayer. This is not wrong, but we should seek the peace and the comfort of His Spirit during our prayers of supplication. Humble requests do not seek to be answered in our way, but rather in His way.

It is also worth noting that prayers of supplication are not for ourselves alone. We are admonished by the Word to be praying for others as well. Paul gives specific directions to Timothy and the church in Ephesus for whom to pray. He states, "First of all, then, I urge that supplications, prayers, intercessions, and thanksgivings be made for all people, for kings and all who are in high positions" (1 Tim. 2:1-2).

We are to be praying for all people, but most importantly, for those who lead us, all the way to the President of the United States. No matter who is in office, we are to offer prayers of supplication for them. Whether we agree with the president or not does not matter one bit. We are called to humbly pray for him.

---

[50] A. W. Tozer and Ron Eggert, *Tozer for the Christian Leader: A 365-Day Devotional* (Chicago: Moody Publishers, 2015), 17.

PRAYERS OF INTERCESSION ARE INTERVENTIONS ON BEHALF OF OTHERS (JOHN 17; NUM. 14; ROM. 8:26-28).

In His prayer in John 17, Jesus interceded for His disciples. He prayed earnestly for their sanctification and protection. He asked the Father to keep them protected, so they could grow in their faith. Jesus then also prayed for the salvation of others, as well as the protection of those who would believe. We see the role of the priests in the Old Testament as intercessors who would sacrifice animals for the sake of the sins of the people. Today, we are to sacrifice time to intercede for others.

Intercession is praying for those who do not or will not pray for themselves. Intercessory prayer is, in a sense, going to bat for others. We stand between God and them and beg Him to spare them or bring them to salvation or to bring healing. We can pray for the Lord's mercy for those who would not ask for mercy themselves.

Jesus did this on the cross for those who were sinning against Him. He declared, "'They know not what they do'" (Luke 23:34). This was an intercessory prayer. Moses did this for the people of Israel when God's wrath was focused on them. Moses stood in the gap for the Israelites, even in the middle of their utter disobedience.

Intercession is different from supplication because it is a prayer of intervention, not simply a request for help. In Romans 8, we see that the Holy Spirit Himself intercedes for us. Some prayers done in the Spirit are intercessions for ourselves for which the Spirit is giving us utterance. We will see more soon on the prayers in the Spirit.

PRAYERS OF THANKSGIVING RECOGNIZE THE GIVER IS GOOD (PHIL. 4:6; 1 TIM. 2:1-2; 1 TIM. 4:4-5; 1 THESS. 5:18)

Every good gift comes from above, and we are to offer prayers of thanksgiving to the Lord for His goodness. We recognize not only the gift, but also the Giver. Constantly remembering from what He has rescued us, the things that He gives (like our daily bread), and the reality that everything in life is a gift help reframe our mind. When we offer thanksgiving, it is hard to feel entitled. When we offer thanksgiving, it is difficult to be prideful for what we have. Giving thanks helps refocus our hearts and minds on the Giver and helps dispel our anxiety.

"Give thanks in all circumstances" (1 Thess. 5:18) helps remind us that the Lord is bigger than anything else this world may throw at us. Prayers of thanksgiving can even make unclean things clean (1 Tim. 4:4-5). Prayers of thanksgiving turn our hearts from grumbling to rejoicing. These types of prayers erase our worries and bring freedom from anxiety because we see the goodness of the Giver.

There are many ways of prayer that Scripture lays out. This week, we can remember it through the acronym **SIT**. We believers **SIT** to pray. We can pray in **S**upplication, **I**ntercession, and **T**hanksgiving. Prayer also has a component of listening, as does all good communication. As we look at navigation lighting, we will see how we can hear the voice of God and use His Word as a lighthouse to lead us home.

KEY TAKEAWAY PRINCIPLES

- If one communication method does not work, try a different one.
- Know your audience—they may prefer a specific form of communication.
- Listen!

There are many different ways to communicate with God.

FURTHER STUDY

- "Therefore I tell you, whatever you ask in prayer, believe that you have received it, and it will be yours" (Mark 11:24).

- "Pray without ceasing" (1 Thess. 5:17).
- "If we confess our sins, he is faithful and just to forgive us our sins and to cleanse us from all unrighteousness" (1 John 1:9).
- "Casting all your anxieties on him, because he cares for you" (1 Peter 5:7).

CHAPTER 12
NAVIGATION LIGHTING

When operating a vessel between sunset and sunrise, it is important to have navigation lighting. Generally, navigation lights include red and green sidelights. Green indicates the starboard side, and red indicates the port side. Some vessels may also be required to have mast lights and stern lights.

The most popular navigation lighting is not even on a ship; it is from a lighthouse. Lighthouses generally have a special meaning in Christianity because they represent guidance, refuge, and salvation. They can also symbolize overcoming challenges and navigating through the adversities of the world.

In Psalm 119:105, we read the psalmist's words, "Your word is a lamp to my feet and a light to my path." Nothing in our Christian walk could be more of a lighthouse for the navigation of our souls than God's Word. Yet it is not simply the written Word to which we are to pay attention. Another form of prayer is listening. As we read the Word, the Spirit also speaks the Word to our hearts.

STUDY FIRST
Read Acts 1:8, 13:1-4.

This passage captures the picture of God speaking and a group of believers (leaders, no less) taking time to listen, seeing the light to their path, and then sailing into obedience following the path the Lord's light sets.

I would say that my sense of hearing is one of my most underutilized senses. My wife may even say it is a "neglected" sense. I am not sure what it is, but I simply have trouble consistently hearing her. I may be distracted by the text I received, the kid bouncing on the couch, or the television show I am watching; but I find myself missing much of what she and others say to me.

Many times, I recognize I am zoned into something else and am not expecting her (or my kids) to speak to me, so I miss it. I may hear them speaking like the *Peanuts* mom in the background; but I do not anticipate what they are saying is for me at all, so I simply do not hear what is being said. I am working on this because it is vital to a healthy relationship to hear and actually listen.

I fear I do this same deficient hearing when it comes to the Lord, and I would venture to guess many of you do as well. I fear many live their lives as if God has spoken but not as if He is currently speaking. Many of us simply think God's Word is the spoken Word of God, and we live as if that is all we need. However, there is more to His speaking! If this is the case, how can we tune ourselves into hearing His voice?

I believe the passage of Scripture we have read can answer that very question. These prophets and teachers came with an expectant heart to have intimacy with God and to hear His voice. So, to tune into His voice, there are a few things we need to do.

EXPECTING GOD TO SPEAK SETS US UP TO LISTEN (ACTS 13:1-2)

In this passage, we see a group of "prophets and teachers" as well as the whole congregation with them gathering to worship and fast. This type of intentional worship and fasting in the New Testament was typically done to hear the Lord speak on a topic. This was a service of intentionally pressing in with the expectation of hearing God speak—not on a specific topic, as that is not suggested in the text, but rather to experience intimacy with God.

They were not only expectant but also had a level of "holy desperation" to be close to God. They came expecting a word from God. It was not simply a time to gather and sing but a time of deep intentionality and expectation. The Western Christian has lost much of their expectancy. A sense of having an intimate two-way conversation with God is one sense that seems to be largely missing. As I stated before, a healthy relationship has a sense of listening involved in it. We cannot just do all the talking. How often are we personally coming with this sense of expectancy? When we go to church or open our Bibles, how often are we expecting Him to speak directly to us?

A.W. Tozer once said, "Some Christians memorize the Word of God but never meet the God who wrote the Word. They can quote whole chapters but have never been inspired by the same Holy Spirit that inspired the Word."[51] The Holy Spirit desires to make the Word come alive to us. He desires to speak through the Word and cause it to bring transformation to our lives, not simply education for our minds. In fact, John 16:13 states, "When the Spirit of truth comes, he will guide you into all the truth, for he will not speak on his own authority, but whatever he hears he will speak, and he will declare to you the things that are to come."

Jesus declared to us that as we read truth, the Spirit of truth would guide us in all the truth we encounter! He emphatically declares that the Holy Spirit will be *speaking*. We must expect Him to speak. Expectancy is very important to actually hearing.

If one expects a package or a message to come, they are eagerly waiting for it to ensure they do not miss it. When one is not expecting a package or a message to come, they live as if nothing is going to change, so they often miss that package or message. I, for one, do not desire to miss out on the speaking voice of God. His message will come no matter what because He is a speaking God, but if I am not available to the Word, He speaks due to my lack of expectancy. The lack of hearing is on me. The lack of hearing rooted in a lack of expectancy is our failure, not God's.

Many of us may simply read the Bible to click the checkbox on our app or the website (or maybe even a paper copy) declaring we have done today's reading. Maybe at this point, some of us have lost our expectancy to hear from

---

51   Tozer, *Tozer*, 54.

God and are simply going through the motions. I challenge you to allow the Spirit of God to reawaken your expectancy. God has a fresh Word in season for us all! Take time to earnestly seek what He desires to declare to you each day you read. Ask the Spirit of God to illuminate the Word to you each morning and do not allow the enemy to trick you into thinking it is just reading because it is not!

As we look at this church and how they approached hearing from God, they did not simply expect God to appear; they gathered together with a communal expectation.

SEEK THE LORD'S VOICE IN COMMUNITY (ACTS 13:1-4)

Notice that they gathered together as believers to worship, fast, and pray. They may have done this on their own. In fact, I suspect they did, but here we see them doing so corporately. When it comes to hearing from the Lord, it is not just an individual task, it is a corporate one.

The eclectic group that was united under the banner of Christ were together seeking Him. There, all of them heard the voice of the Lord say, "'Set apart for me Barnabas and Saul'" (Acts 13:2). This audible voice from Heaven is not a normal occurrence, but the point is still clear: we are to seek the Lord, His direction, and His voice both on our own and together.

Church is not just a hangout. It is a setting for hearing from the Lord. When we worship, pray, and hear the Word together, we should be seeking to hear from the Lord both for ourselves and for our church as a whole. Maybe during the pandemic, you found yourself alone and stopped gathering with the body of believers. Let us encourage you to *go back* to community! We were not meant to walk the Christian life together. Get over fear. Get out of the lazy rut. Stop making excuses and get into community.

As we look at this church and how they approached hearing from God, they did not simply expect God to show up. They sacrificially sought after the voice of God.

BEING SACRIFICIAL IN OUR SEARCH TO HEAR HIS VOICE OPENS OUR EARS

These prophets and teachers were leading a congregation in a time of fasting. The Greek work used here does mean to abstain from eating and was voluntary. It was the people's desire to abstain from the pleasures and nourishment of food to hear God speak. They sacrificed food. They were also in an extended time of worship. There is no sense of how long they were fasting and worshiping, but one can assume that they were doing both long enough at the same time for the idea of fasting to mean anything. They were not simply skipping lunch and worshiping while they missed a meal. There was a significant sacrifice of time, energy, and food.

In today's culture, we have everything easy, so I fear we often expect hearing God's voice to be just as quick and easy. Yet sometimes, there is a need for a sacrifice of time for prayer, worship, and fasting to transpire to show God how much you desire the intimacy of His voice. In our society, sacrifice is not an often-desired word we use. We do not like to sacrifice unless it somehow benefits us.

Too often, we want God's answers without sacrifice and without intimacy. God does not work that way, just as no human does either. In this passage, we see a diverse community coming together to sacrifice to hear His voice. They recognize that only God's voice matters. Only His way is the way, so they press in and wait upon the Lord to hear His voice.

This type of sacrificially waiting upon the Lord not only allows us to hear His voice, but it also changes us. As Tozer once said, "If we just stopped all our busyness; got quiet, worshiped God, and waited on Him;[sic] we would rise above the carnality of present Christians."[52] God would literally shift the atmosphere around us. We would hear Him speak. His direction would come. His guidance would lead us. He would show us where we are to go.

Yet we neglect this type of intimacy with God. Maybe we do not desire to go where He wants us to go, or maybe we believe that God is no longer

---

52   Ibid, 74.

speaking to us. Yet I assure you, He is speaking and desires to speak to all of us.

As we look at this church and how they approached hearing from God, we see they sacrificially sought after the voice of God.

WE MUST BE WILLING TO OBEY HIS VOICE (ACTS 13:3-4)

God spoke to this group in Acts. This moment was the life-changing moment for both Paul and the Church itself (not just Antioch). The Holy Spirit spoke clearly and gave direction in His speaking.

God had called out Paul and Barnabas to a specific task. They had been doing great work in Antioch. God had been using them mightily. They were both listed in the group of "prophets and teachers." This church had to make another sacrifice in obeying the voice of God. They had to let two of their best go so those two could bless every nation.

Sometimes, as a corporate body, we must send away our best people. We are to be a sending movement, after all. Sometimes, that may look like sending people to Samaria. Sometimes, it means sending people to the ends of the earth. Either way, the church is called to send, and sending can hurt. However, as Acts 1:8 reminds us, the Holy Spirit is our empowerment; and where God guides, God provides!

Obeying the voice of God is not always easy, but it is always the best course to take. When we take expectant and sacrificial time to hear His voice, we will hear Him speak. We may not always like what He says, nor will we always jump at the chance to obey His voice—but obey we must.

What does this have to do with missions? Well, we are all *called* to go, send, and pray. As we tune our hearts to the Lord, we must seek to ask, *Where am I to go? Whom am I to send? And how am I to pray?*

God truly is a speaking God. God is truly lighting lamps and lighthouses for our safe navigation in life. We the people of God need to regain our desire to hear Him speak, as well as seek intimacy with Him. Let us resolve to take off our earmuffs of unexpectancy and unbelief and again sacrificially seek a deeper life in Him. God desires to speak to us. Will we listen? Will we obediently follow the trajectory to which He is pointing us?

KEY TAKEAWAY PRINCIPLES

- Understand the importance of lighting.
- The color of lights can make a huge difference in life.
- What navigation lights and beacons do you trust in your life?

FURTHER STUDY

- "Again Jesus spoke to them, saying, 'I am the light of the world. Whoever follows me will not walk in darkness, but will have the light of life'" (John 8:12).
- "The LORD is my light and my salvation; whom shall I fear? The LORD is the stronghold of my life; of whom shall I be afraid?" (Psalm 27:1).
- "In the same way, let your light shine before others, so that they may see your good works and give glory to your Father who is in heaven" (Matt. 5:16).

CHAPTER 13
WIDOW'S NET

The widow's net is a safety precaution to catch crew members who are out beyond the bow of the ship. It is there to protect the sailors. When the ship is under sail, it is also a nice place to relax and watch the bow of the ship as it cuts through the waves.

Sometimes, we take things too far. Whether it is our estimation of our own capabilities or a joke that crosses the line, we simply take it further than we should. In my perspective, we can never go too far when it comes to our pursuit of God, but there are many other areas where we do not know where to draw the line. We can allow our minds to wander to areas they should not. We can allow a sin pattern to continue and cause a bigger mess than if we had dealt with it earlier. We can consistently put ourselves in precarious scenarios where we then fall off the ship.

When I think of a widow's net, I tend to see accountability. Some might see it as simply a safety net, something they know will catch them if and when they fall. This mentality flirts with disaster, in my opinion, and we should see the widow's net as more of a structure put in place to be a boundary, not a safety net.

In this instance, I am seeing a boundary as something that helps a person steer clear of crossing the line. Instead of it encouraging someone to flirt with disaster, it is a warning bell of imminent death if crossed. For example, a boundary for a young couple who are seeking to remain abstinent would be, "We will not be alone past eleven p.m." If the goal is to stay out of the waters of sexual intimacy until marriage, the boundary is the widow's net put in place to ensure that does not happen.

Therefore, a boundary is not a line with which to flirt but rather a systemically, purposefully, and strategically designed structure to help a person not "cross the line." Too often, flirting with the line generally leads to disaster. Henry Cloud, the author of *Boundaries: When to Say Yes, How to Say No to Take Control of Your Life*, once said:

> Boundaries help us keep the good in and the bad out. Setting boundaries inevitably involves taking responsibility for your choices. You are the one who makes them. You are the one who must live with their consequences. And you are the one who may be keeping yourself from making the choices you could be happy with. We must own our own thoughts and clarify distorted thinking.[53]

We all need a good widow's net set up in our lives. No one wants to go overboard. One thing we must do is invite the Spirit of the Living God to speak into the nets we need to set up—how to set them up and where to set them up. You may want to set up a widow's net in the back of the ship; but you never go there, so that net is not as important as the net set up to create a boundary when you are tempted to fall. Only through the Holy Spirit can you discern where the net needs to go.

You could also set up a net with huge holes in it, rendering it useless. You need the Holy Spirit to guide you in the type of net you need. Also, we have different seasons in our lives. That young dating couple will cut the net of eleven p.m. out of their lives when they get married. So, we will have to lean on the Spirit as to when the nets need to be set up as well.

Again, we all need widow's nets. I encourage you to continue growing in your faith and in your holiness. A well-placed, well-timed, and

---

[53] Henry Cloud and John Sims Townsend, *Boundaries: When to Say Yes, How to Say No to Take Control of Your Life* (Grand Rapids: Zondervan, 2017), 248.

well-put-together widow's net on the ship of your life will help in this continued growth. Trust me!

KEY TAKEAWAY PRINCIPLES

- There is a safety net for mankind.
- Be secure in your safety and future.
- It is okay to anticipate possible problems in your future.

FURTHER STUDY

- "And so also were James and John, sons of Zebedee, who were partners with Simon. And Jesus said to Simon, 'Do not be afraid; from now on you will be catching men'" (Luke 5:10).
- "The Lord is my light and my salvation; whom shall I fear? The Lord is the stronghold of my life; of whom shall I be afraid?" (Psalm 27:1).
- "Guarding the paths of justice and watching over the way of his saints" (Prov. 2:8).

CHAPTER 14
FIGUREHEAD

The figurehead is a carving on the bow of a ship. Figureheads existed during biblical times. At the bow of a ship, there would be a wood carving displaying something of importance. Common examples included gods, women, coats of arms, and owners. The Phoenicians were some of the first people to use figureheads.

What is most important to your life? Or should I ask *who* is most important? It is true that many times, we can put up false "figureheads" that we simply want people to think are the best or most important things about us, but we really do talk and live out what we believe. The words and actions we consistently display in public and in private speak volumes as to what we believe. Your life tells the story of your beliefs.

I bring this up under the idea of "figurehead" because the figurehead identified the ship. If the god Poseidon was there, they were identifying as Greeks who worshipped a god of the sea and desired to serve him well enough to not have trouble at sea. They wanted to raise up Poseidon, so he would raise them up in safety.

Sometimes, the word "figurehead" is used to say that someone is out front, but they are really not the one in charge. What if Christ was not only the Figurehead but also the One really in charge? What if we chose to put Him out front and actually let Him lead the ship instead of arresting control back from Him whenever we felt like it?

After all, we cannot control God, no matter how often we like to think we can. Our ship should be known by Him at the head of the ship and at the helm of the ship. Let it be so.

KEY TAKEAWAY PRINCIPLES

- Understand what is important to people.
- Who is your figurehead?

FURTHER STUDY

- "After three months we set sail in a ship that had wintered in the island, a ship of Alexandria, with the twin gods as a figurehead" (Acts 28:11).
- "And God spoke all these words, saying, 'I am the Lord your God, who brought you out of the land of Egypt, out of the house of slavery. 'You shall have no other gods before me. 'You shall not make for yourself a carved image, or any likeness of anything that is in heaven above, or that is in the earth beneath, or that is in the water under the earth. You shall not bow down to them or serve them, for I the Lord your God am a jealous God, visiting the iniquity of the fathers on the children to the third and the fourth generation of those who hate me" (Exod. 20:1-5).

PART 2
NAUTICAL TERMINOLOGY AND SAYINGS

BY: TIM HIBSMAN

CHAPTER 15
NAUTICAL SLOGANS AND SAYINGS

STAY THE COURSE

Definition: You must maintain your heading. We all have different objectives, goals, and missions when it comes to family, career, education, and especially our Christian journey. There will be stumbling blocks, but it is important to stay on course and keep the faith.

RELATED VERSES:

- "Blessed are those whose way is blameless, who walk in the law of the LORD!" (Psalm 119:1).
- "I have fought the good fight, I have finished the race, I have kept the faith" (2 Tim. 4:7).

BATTEN DOWN THE HATCHES

Definition: Secure for hard times. You should be prepared for hard times.

RELATED VERSES:

- "God is our refuge and strength, a very present help in trouble. Therefore, we will not fear though the earth gives way, though the mountains be moved into the heart of the sea, though its waters roar and foam, though the mountains tremble at its swelling" (Psalm 46:1-3).
- "Preach the word; be ready in season and out of season; reprove, rebuke, and exhort, with complete patience and teaching" (2 Tim. 4:2).

CUT AND RUN

Definition: Run away. This probably comes from ships making a hasty departure by cutting the anchor rope and running with the wind. Avoid trouble. Sometimes, it is necessary to run away from a dangerous situation.

RELATED VERSES:

- "The prudent sees danger and hides himself, but the simple go on and suffer for it" (Prov. 22:3).
- "Flee from sexual immorality. Every other sin a person commits is outside the body, but the sexually immoral person sins against his own body" (1 Cor. 6:18).
- "But as for you, O man of God, flee these things. Pursue righteousness, godliness, faith, love, steadfastness, gentleness" (1 Tim. 6:11).

GET UNDERWAY

Definition: Begin a voyage. Getting started is sometimes the hardest part. Untying the rope from the security of the dock may push your vessel into the unstable seas.

RELATED VERSES:

- "And though your beginning was small, your latter days will be very great" (Job 8:7).
- "Behold, I am doing a new thing; now it springs forth, do you not perceive it? I will make a way in the wilderness and rivers in the desert" (Isa. 43:19).

GIVE A WIDE BERTH

Definition: Sometimes, you need to keep a clear distance from trouble.

RELATED VERSES:

- "Avoid it; do not go on it; turn away from it and pass on" (Prov. 4:15).

- "I appeal to you, brothers, to watch out for those who cause divisions and create obstacles contrary to the doctrine that you have been taught; avoid them" (Rom. 16:17).
- "It will never be inhabited or lived in for all generations; no Arab will pitch his tent there; no shepherds will make their flocks lie down there" (Isa. 13:20).

KNOW THE ROPES

Definition: Understand the principles. Before you play a game, you must understand the rules. Before you leap into a new job, you must be trained.

RELATED VERSES:

- "All Scripture is breathed out by God and profitable for teaching, for reproof, for correction, and for training in righteousness" (2 Tim. 3:16).
- "In the beginning was the Word, and the Word was with God, and the Word was God" (John 1:1).
- "If you keep my commandments, you will abide in my love, just as I have kept my Father's commandments and abide in his love" (John 15:10).

EVEN KEELED

Definition: The boat floats upright without listing. The keel is the longitudinal structure along the centerline at the bottom of a vessel's hull on which the rest of the hull is built. It is important to be steadfast and calm in your Christian journey.

RELATED VERSES:

- "Therefore, my beloved brothers, be steadfast, immovable, always abounding in the work of the Lord, knowing that in the Lord your labor is not in vain" (1 Cor. 15:58).

- "Blessed is the man who remains steadfast under trial, for when he has stood the test he will receive the crown of life, which God has promised to those who love him" (James 1:12).
- "Count it all joy, my brothers, when you meet trials of various kinds, for you know that the testing of your faith produces steadfastness. And let steadfastness have its full effect, that you may be perfect and complete, lacking in nothing" (James 1:2-4).
- "Older men are to be sober-minded, dignified, self-controlled, sound in faith, in love, and in steadfastness" (Titus 2:2).

KEEL OVER

Definition: This term means to fall over or a sailor's term for dying or stumbling. When the boat's keel comes out of the water, it is very likely to capsize. Staying strong and faithful is the key. However, there are times when people stumble. It is common to be shaken up, just like a ship tossed around in a storm.

RELATED VERSES:

- "It is good not to eat meat or drink wine or do anything that causes your brother to stumble" (Rom. 14:21).
- "But take care that this right of yours does not somehow become a stumbling block to the weak" (1 Cor. 8:9).
- "As you come to him, a living stone rejected by men but in the sight of God chosen and precious, you yourselves like living stones are being built up as a spiritual house, to be a holy priesthood, to offer spiritual sacrifices acceptable to God through Jesus Christ. For it stands in Scripture: 'Behold, I am laying in Zion a stone, a cornerstone chosen and precious, and whoever believes in him will not be put to shame.' So the honor is for you who believe, but for those who do not believe, 'The stone that the builders

rejected has become the cornerstone,' and 'A stone of stumbling, and a rock of offense.' They stumble because they disobey the word, as they were destined to do. But you are a chosen race, a royal priesthood, a holy nation, a people for his own possession, that you may proclaim the excellencies of him who called you out of darkness into his marvelous light. Once you were not a people, but now you are God's people; once you had not received mercy, but now you have received mercy. Beloved, I urge you as sojourners and exiles to abstain from the passions of the flesh, which wage war against your soul. Keep your conduct among the Gentiles honorable, so that when they speak against you as evildoers, they may see your good deeds and glorify God on the day of visitation" (1 Peter 2:4-12).

HOMEPORT

Definition: The port from which your voyage began is your homeport. Home is a word that is usually synonymous with peace, rest, security, and comfort.

RELATED VERSES:
- "My people will abide in a peaceful habitation, in secure dwellings, and in quiet resting places" (Isa. 32:18).
- "By wisdom a house is built, and by understanding it is established; by knowledge the rooms are filled with all precious and pleasant riches" (Prov. 24:3-4).
- "Whatever house you enter, first say, 'Peace be to this house!'" (Luke 10:5).
- "In the house of the righteous there is much treasure, but trouble befalls the income of the wicked" (Prov. 15:6).
- "'I have indeed built you an exalted house, a place for you to dwell in forever'" (1 Kings 8:13).

PIPE DOWN

Definition: This is a request for silence. The boatswain's pipe was used to give signals to the crew of sailing ships. "Piping down the hammocks" was the last signal of the day to go below decks and retire for the night. Being quiet is mentioned often in the Bible. When you are silent or quiet, it often means you are reflecting on and understanding the situation. This is opposed to someone who is emotional, boisterous, and disruptive.

RELATED VERSES:

- "'The LORD will fight for you, and you have only to be silent'" (Exod. 14:14).
- "'Be still, and know that I am God. I will be exalted among the nations, I will be exalted in the earth!'" (Psalm 46:10).
- "Whoever belittles his neighbor lacks sense, but a man of understanding remains silent" (Prov. 11:12).
- "When words are many, transgression is not lacking, but whoever restrains his lips is prudent" (Prov. 10:19).

THREE SHEETS TO THE WIND

Definition: This term is used to describe someone who is very drunk. In sailors' language, a sheet is a rope. If three sheets are not attached to the sails as they ought to be, the sail will flap, and the boat will lurch around in a drunken fashion. Sailors had a sliding scale of drunkenness. Tipsy was "one sheet," whereas falling over was "three sheets." There are several obstacles in the Christian journey. These temptations are addressed by the Bible, especially when it comes to alcohol.

RELATED VERSES:

- "And do not get drunk with wine, for that is debauchery, but be filled with the Spirit" (Eph. 5:18).
- "Wine is a mocker, strong drink a brawler, and whoever is led astray by it is not wise" (Prov. 20:1).

- "Woe to those who rise early in the morning, that they may run after strong drink, who tarry late into the evening as wine inflames them!" (Isa. 5:11).
- "Woe to those who are heroes at drinking wine, and valiant men in mixing strong drink" (Isa. 5:22).

LOGBOOK

Definition: A logbook records official information. There is no other record book more important than the Book of Life.

RELATED VERSES:
- "The one who conquers will be clothed thus in white garments, and I will never blot his name out of the book of life. I will confess his name before my Father and before his angels" (Rev. 3:5).
- "And if anyone's name was not found written in the book of life, he was thrown into the lake of fire" (Rev. 20:15).
- "And all who dwell on earth will worship it, everyone whose name has not been written before the foundation of the world in the book of life of the Lamb who was slain" (Rev. 13:8).
- "'Nevertheless, do not rejoice in this, that the spirits are subject to you, but rejoice that your names are written in heaven'" (Luke 10:20).
- "Yes, I ask you also, true companion, help these women, who have labored side by side with me in the gospel together with Clement and the rest of my fellow workers, whose names are in the book of life" (Phil. 4:3).

HAND OVER FIST

Definition: It describes the action of hauling on a rope using alternate hands very quickly and continuously. Pulling the ropes is physically demanding and often associated with hard work.

RELATED VERSE:

- "Whatever you do, work heartily, as for the Lord and not for men" (Col. 3:23).
- "For even when we were with you, we would give you this command: If anyone is not willing to work, let him not eat. For we hear that some among you walk in idleness, not busy at work, but busybodies. Now such persons we command and encourage in the Lord Jesus Christ to do their work quietly and to earn their own living" (2 Thess. 3:10-12).

DEAD IN THE WATER

Definition: A ship that is "dead in the water" has no wind in its sails to make it come alive and was therefore not able to move forward. A ship that is dead in the water has no movement forward, similar to death. It is important to avoid standing still in your faith and move forward in the Spirit.

RELATED VERSES:

- "So we are always of good courage. We know that while we are at home in the body we are away from the Lord, for we walk by faith, not by sight. Yes, we are of good courage, and we would rather be away from the body and at home with the Lord" (2 Cor. 5:6-8).
- "'For I have no pleasure in the death of anyone, declares the Lord God; so turn, and live'" (Ezek. 18:32).
- "And I heard a voice from heaven saying, 'Write this: Blessed are the dead who die in the LORD from now on.' 'Blessed indeed,' says the Spirit,' 'that they may rest from their labors, for their deeds follow them!'" (Rev. 14:13).

OVER A BARREL

Definition: The most common form of punishment for sailors was flogging. The culprit was tied either to a grating, the mast, or over a barrel.

"Kissing the gunner's daughter" was being tied to the barrel of a deck cannon while it was fired. Being over a barrel means being in a tough situation. Several biblical figures were in tough situations.

RELATED VERSES:
- "He said, 'Take your son, your only son Isaac, whom you love, and go to the land of Moriah, and offer him there as a burnt offering on one of the mountains of which I shall tell you'" (Gen. 22:2).
- "Now the word of the LORD came to Jonah the son of Amittai, saying, 'Arise, go to Nineveh, that great city, and call out against it, for their evil has come up before me.' But Jonah rose to flee to Tarshish from the presence of the LORD. He went down to Joppa and found a ship going to Tarshish. So he paid the fare and went down into it, to go with them to Tarshish, away from the presence of the LORD" (Jonah 1:1-3).
- Jesus answered, "Will you lay down your life for me? Truly, truly, I say to you, the rooster will not crow till you have denied me three times" (John 13:38).

SHAKE A LEG

Definition: Rouse yourself and get out of bed. "Show a leg" seems to have been the Royal Navy command for putting a foot out of your hammock and getting up. Get out of bed and get some work done.

RELATED VERSES:
- "What good is it, my brothers, if someone says he has faith but does not have works? Can that faith save him? If a brother or sister is poorly clothed and lacking in daily food, and one of you says to them, 'Go in peace, be warmed and filled,' without giving them the things needed for the body, what good is that? So also faith by itself, if it does not have works, is dead. But someone will say, 'You have faith and I have works.' Show me your faith apart

from your works, and I will show you my faith by my works. You believe that God is one; you do well. Even the demons believe—and shudder! Do you want to be shown, you foolish person, that faith apart from works is useless? Was not Abraham our father justified by works when he offered up his son Isaac on the altar? You see that faith was active along with his works, and faith was completed by his works" (James 2:14-22).

- "And let our people learn to devote themselves to good works, so as to help cases of urgent need, and not be unfruitful" (Titus 3:14).

- "The saying is trustworthy, and I want you to insist on these things, so that those who have believed in God may be careful to devote themselves to good works. These things are excellent and profitable for people" (Titus 3:8).

- "Do you want to be shown, you foolish person, that faith apart from works is useless? Was not Abraham our father justified by works when he offered up his son Isaac on the altar? You see that faith was active along with his works, and faith was completed by his works; and the Scripture was fulfilled that says, 'Abraham believed God, and it was counted to him as righteousness'—and he was called a friend of God. You see that a person is justified by works and not by faith alone" (James 2:20-24).

SHIVER MY TIMBERS

Definition: This oath expresses annoyance or surprise. Being surprised by God happens quite often. There are many examples in Scripture where God surprised people.

RELATED VERSES:

- "And Mary said to the angel, 'How will this be, since I am a virgin?'" (Luke 1:34).

- "But Saul, still breathing threats and murder against the disciples of the Lord, went to the high priest and asked him for letters to the synagogues at Damascus, so that if he found any belonging to the Way, men or women, he might bring them bound to Jerusalem. Now as he went on his way, he approached Damascus, and suddenly a light from heaven shone around him. And falling to the ground, he heard a voice saying to him, 'Saul, Saul, why are you persecuting me?' And he said, 'Who are you, Lord?' And he said, 'I am Jesus, whom you are persecuting'" (Acts 9:1-5).
- "Jesus said to her, 'Do not cling to me, for I have not yet ascended to the Father; but go to my brothers and say to them, *I am ascending to my Father and your Father, to my God and your God*'" (John 20:17).

TAKE THE WIND OUT OF HIS SAILS

Definition: This phrase means to take away someone's initiative or to disconcert or frustrate them. This could derive from the art of sailing so that you "steal" the wind from another boat. If someone does not have wind in their sails, they could be sluggish, lazy, frustrated, or lack motivation.

RELATED VERSES:

- "A slack hand causes poverty, but the hand of the diligent makes rich" (Prov. 10:4).
- "The desire of the sluggard kills him, for his hands refuse to labor" (Prov. 21:25).
- "Slothfulness casts into a deep sleep, and an idle person will suffer hunger" (Prov. 19:15).

TOUCH AND GO

Definition: This refers to the situation in which a vessel would be caught in shallow water when it touched the bottom but did not become grounded and was able to move off again. Touch and go means the ship is struggling in shallow water. Struggling is part of the Christian life.

RELATED VERSES:

- "But he said to me, 'My grace is sufficient for you, for my power is made perfect in weakness.' Therefore I will boast all the more gladly of my weaknesses, so that the power of Christ may rest upon me. For the sake of Christ, then, I am content with weaknesses, insults, hardships, persecutions, and calamities. For when I am weak, then I am strong" (2 Cor. 12:9-10).
- "No temptation has overtaken you that is not common to man. God is faithful, and he will not let you be tempted beyond your ability, but with the temptation he will also provide the way of escape, that you may be able to endure it" (1 Cor. 10:13).
- "Not only that, but we rejoice in our sufferings, knowing that suffering produces endurance, and endurance produces character, and character produces hope, and hope does not put us to shame, because God's love has been poured into our hearts through the Holy Spirit who has been given to us" (Rom. 5:3-5).

A SQUARE MEAL

Definition: It was common that wooden plates were square in the days of the tall ships. It was important to get three square meals a day of nutritional food to physically complete your job effectively.

RELATED VERSES:

- "So, whether you eat or drink, or whatever you do, do all to the glory of God" (1 Cor. 10:31).
- "For anyone who eats and drinks without discerning the body eats and drinks judgment on himself" (1 Cor. 11:29).

- "And day by day, attending the temple together and breaking bread in their homes, they received their food with glad and generous hearts" (Acts 2:46).

LOOSE CANNON

Definition: An unpredictable or uncontrolled person is likely to cause unintentional damage. When a cannon breaks loose from its lashings, it can be very dangerous and difficult to get back into its secure spot. A loose cannon can be a lot of trouble.

RELATED VERSES:

- "'Let not your hearts be troubled. Believe in God; believe also in me'" (John 14:1).
- "Casting all your anxieties on him, because he cares for you" (1 Peter 5:7).
- "This poor man cried, and the LORD heard him and saved him out of all his troubles" (Psalm 34:6).

TOE THE LINE

Definition: When the ship's crew were being assembled on the deck, they would line up with their toes all touching a given seam (or line) of the deck planking. This has come to mean accepting authority, principles, or policies of a particular person or group. Toeing the line for God might mean being obedient to one's call.

RELATED VERSES:

- "Let every person be subject to the governing authorities. For there is no authority except from God, and those that exist have been instituted by God" (Rom. 13:1).
- "Whoever spares the rod hates his son, but he who loves him is diligent to discipline him" (Prov. 13:24).

- "Whatever you do, work heartily, as for the Lord and not for men" (Col. 3:23).

A CLEAN BILL OF HEALTH

Definition: In the eighteenth century, a bill of health was an official certificate given to the master of a ship on leaving port, declaring there were no infections on board. After extended time at sea, sometimes the ship and crew were a little less than hygienic. When entering a port, sometimes the authorities would require a certificate attesting that there were no infectious diseases among the ship's crew.

RELATED VERSES:

- "Beloved, I pray that all may go well with you and that you may be in good health, as it goes well with your soul" (3 John 1:2).
- "And he went throughout all Galilee, teaching in their synagogues and proclaiming the gospel of the kingdom and healing every disease and every affliction among the people" (Matt. 4:23).
- "When he went ashore he saw a great crowd, and he had compassion on them and healed their sick" (Matt. 14:14).

WHISTLE FOR THE WIND

Definition: This possibly derives from the nautical superstition that the wind could be summoned to help a becalmed vessel by whistling for it. Sometimes, it feels as if you are in an impossible situation. Calling on God for help is one of the first things that should be done.

RELATED VERSES:

- "I can do all things through him who strengthens me" (Phil. 4:13).
- "Whatever you ask in my name, this I will do, that the Father may be glorified in the Son. If you ask me anything in my name, I will do it" (John 14:13-14).

- "My help comes from the Lord, who made heaven and earth" (Psalm 121:2).
- "'Ask, and it will be given to you; seek, and you will find; knock, and it will be opened to you" (Matt. 7:7).
- "Come to me, all who labor and are heavy laden, and I will give you rest" (Matt. 11:28).
- "Fear not, for I am with you; be not dismayed, for I am your God; I will strengthen you, I will help you, I will uphold you with my righteous right hand" (Isa. 41:10).

PART 3
COMMAND ISSUES AND OFFICERS' DUTIES

Some people are born to lead; some people are born to follow; and some people have leadership thrust upon them. We all have moments of leadership and command responsibilities. You may be the head of your household. You may oversee your children. When you drive, you are in command of that vehicle—which is a huge responsibility that most people take for granted.

Picture your own world (family, department, company, coworkers, etc.) as a ship that may move forward or backward and is never permanent. The business or company has a direction. Employees have personal objectives. Stockholders have an eye on profits and earnings. Captains, crew, and financiers of a ship all have a similar relationship to each other—and must function professionally and appropriately to accomplish their mission.

Leadership and command responsibilities are an honor, responsibility, and privilege that should not be taken lightly. If you are a boss, manager, supervisor, or parent, you have a responsibility to your crew, stockholders, owners, society, environment, family, and yourself to act in a proper manner. The following concepts will help you to be a better leader in any environment.

CHAPTER 16
SHARE THE VISION

Where are you headed? What is the mission and objectives of this voyage? Do not let your crew guess. Point it out. Write it down. Say it. If your crew do not agree with the vision, then something has to change.

Almost every business has a vision statement, mission statement, values, and corporate description written in their business plans. There should be no mystery about the direction of the company. If the people know what is important to the organization and the leaders, they may be able to help when an opportunity arises. Every church should also have a clear vision, mission, and statement of faith. Church leaders should occasionally refer to these items to make sure everyone is headed in the right direction. Here are a few quotes to spark some thought:

- "Great Leaders . . . are both highly visionary and highly practical. Their vision enables them to see beyond the immediate."[54]
- "The leader must also live the vision. The leader's effective modeling of the vision makes the picture come alive!"[55]
- "Where there is no prophetic vision the people cast off restraint, but blessed is he who keeps the law" (Prov. 29:18).

In my (Marv) first pastorate, I remember a moment when I first walked into my new office. I sat down in my office chair and began thinking, *I have arrived. My hard work in college has paid off. I am now a pastor.*

---

[54] John C. Maxwell, *The 21 Irrefutable Laws of Leadership: Follow Them and People Will Follow You* (New York: HarperCollins Leadership, 2022), 158.
[55] Ibid, 159.

As I sat there thinking those thoughts, a bigger, more looming thought came to mind. *What is my vision for this ministry?* Right away, my next thought was, *How and where do I begin?* When those thoughts came, I grabbed my journal and simply wrote, *I need your help, Lord; I have no idea what I'm doing!*

Although I had learned how to develop a mission and vision statement during my college years, I still had a hard time. The vision statement I developed in college was a generality. Now, I had to develop a specific vision for a specific ministry. I was stumped and would spend much of that first year stumbling around with the vision and mission of my new ministry. As I talk with younger leaders who have just stepped into ministry, they, too, experience the same type of difficulty as it pertains to vision.

Vision is much like a compass on a trip. It helps determine and maintain the direction of a course. Anything that would seek to take the trip off course is subject to the vision. A detour to the east will hinder a course due north. If the pilot follows the compass, he has an easier time of determining whether a direction will help or hinder the trip. Vision is the same. Everything is subject to the vision. It becomes easier for a leader to determine what will hinder or help the direction of the organization based off the vision. A solid vision gives laser focus, but a weak vision is open to interpretation. Visions that are open for interpretation are a leader's worst nightmare because everything can contend for time or course direction.

If there is no vision, people will go off and do their own thing, and churches and/or organizations will flounder. There must be a unifying vision, or there will be no movement. In the book of Revelation, the apostle John shares with the church in Ephesus how they were doing so many things well, but they had lost the focus and vision of their first love. This loss of vision caused them to flounder and become ineffective. John urged them to get back to the vision.

As well-trained, long-time leaders, you know these truths to be true—not only from a "book knowledge" perspective but also from a very real, experience-driven perspective. As a leader, you have probably experienced several people trying to develop their own vision to help determine the course of your church or organization. You may have inherited a bad vision that continued to get derailed because of its weak nature. As a leader, you know a good vision can be an anchor, so when detractors among your people try to steer the ship off course, you, the leader, can point back to the vision and ask, "Does this direction fit our current vision?"

When a vision is strong, that question can be answered with effectiveness. People will be forced to easily recognize if their course correction is in line with the vision or not. If such a vision does not exist, the person will easily be able to persuade others that it does, in fact, fit the overall vision.

I believe this idea of vision is one that should be a part of every life and not just every corporation or church. Have we developed a vision for our lives? Are we lost adrift in the sea of life because we have neglected to develop what is called a "life's vision"? If vision is so important to keeping an organization or church on track, why would we not use this same helpful tool for our lives? As I have unpacked this year after year, my life's vision statement is "To know God, be known by God, and to make God known." It guides and directs everything I do and helps me to wonder if what I am doing is helping me fulfill this vision or not.

KEY TAKEAWAY PRINCIPLES

- Understand the common goal.
- Have no speculation or confusion.
- The crew can contribute and make suggestions.
- Buy in and receive the treasure at the end.

FURTHER STUDY

- "And the LORD answered me: 'Write the vision; make it plain on tablets, so he may run who reads it' (Hab. 2:2).

- "For I know the plans I have for you, declares the LORD, plans for welfare and not for evil, to give you a future and a hope" (Jer. 29:11).
- "The heart of man plans his way, but the LORD establishes his steps" (Prov. 16:9).
- "Commit your work to the LORD, and your plans will be established" (Prov. 16:3).

CHAPTER 17
PAY ATTENTION TO SIGNS

Any good navigator can recognize the signs of the tides and an oncoming weather change. They are trained in knowing these signs and their meaning. Signs can be good or bad. The navigator could recognize the change from storm to calm or vice versa. If a navigator stops paying attention to these signs, the entire ship will be caught off guard and not ready for the difficulty to come.

In our Christian walk, we will notice warning signs within our souls. First Peter 5:8-9 says, "Be sober-minded; be watchful. Your adversary the devil prowls around like a roaring lion, seeking someone to devour. Resist him, firm in your faith, knowing that the same kinds of suffering are being experienced by your brotherhood throughout the world."

SHEEP ARE TO BE CLEAR MINDED AND ALERT (1 PETER 5:8A)

A consistent and constant theme we will encounter in this letter from start to finish is Peter admonishing the Church "to be ready." The term "sober-minded" was meant to put within the mind of the reader the opposite of drunk. When one is drunk, they are slow at reacting, lost in their intoxication, and not thinking clearly. Peter is admonishing the Church to have a clear and sharp mind.

The commentator Karen Jobes states, "In 1 Peter it refers also to spiritual sobriety, a clear-minded and self-controlled mental state that is free from confusion and driving passions."[56] Also, Peter admonishes the Church to

---

56   Karen H. Jobes, *1 Peter* (Grand Rapids: Baker Academic, 2005), 313.

be alert. We assume the person is clear-minded because one cannot be alert without a sober mind. The Greek word for "be watchful" is the word *gregorayo*, which means "be awake, be on alert, be on the lookout."57 This is military and nautical language for the watchman who would always be ready to spot the enemies' attacks or the dangers ahead of the ship to ensure his group is prepared for defense or a change of course.

Peter then gives the reason: we have an enemy who wants to devour us! He is a roaring lion who quietly pounces on his prey. The imagery is stark. Lions sneak up on their prey; and if the animal is not ready, it *will* be devoured. Sheep cannot be lulled into sleep, and neither can the shepherds who are to give the clarion call of the attack. We must be awake! A sleeping animal is easy prey for a smart and crafty lion.

SHEEP ARE TO RESIST THE DEADLY ALLURE OF THE ENEMY (JAMES 4:7-8; 1 PETER 5:9)

The enemy can seem to have some attraction to him. He masquerades in clothes of light but is of nothing but darkness. The Greek word for "resist" is *anthistemi* and means "to set oneself against." It is the same word James uses when he says, "Resist the devil, and he will flee from you" (1 Peter 5:9). We can do this as Peter says: "firm in our faith." We may believe the lie that we cannot resist the devil, but my brothers and sisters, we *can*! Christ has given us His Spirit in order to resist the devil. He will *have* to flee when we resist him in faith.

In his commentary, Norman Hillyer states, "What are believers to do about the attacks of the devil? They are to resist him, to stand fearlessly up to him. Christians are not to fear the devil, but neither are they to underestimate him."58 We must invite Christ into our fearless battle against the enemy, for without Christ, we will lose. Yet, we *can* win with Christ!

---

57 *Greek-English Lexicon of the New Testament: Based on Semantic Domains*, Vol. 1., J.P. Louw and E. A. Nida, eds., 2nd edition (Swindon: United Bible Societies, 1996), *s.v.* gregorayo.
58 Hillyer, ibid.

To be watchful, then, has a key ingredient—intimacy with Christ. Sometimes, only the Holy Spirit will be able to see the oncoming dangers or blessings. When we spend time with the Lord, we can have the warnings in our hearts that only He can give. It is not a matter of *if* dangers will arise, but *when*. The enemy would love nothing more than to derail a believer, so be ready!

KEY TAKEAWAY PRINCIPLES

- Study the signs and beware of currents, tides, buoys, charts, etc.
- Do not be afraid to delegate duties to provide you with more time to focus on the important issues.
- Learn from the ships and crew traveling before you.

FURTHER STUDY

- "So Jesus said to him, 'Unless you see signs and wonders you will not believe'" (John 4:48).
- "Be sober-minded; be watchful. Your adversary the devil prowls around like a roaring lion, seeking someone to devour" (1 Peter 5:8).
- "As he sat on the Mount of Olives, the disciples came to him privately, saying, 'Tell us, when will these things be, and what will be the sign of your coming and of the end of the age?'" (Matt. 24:3).

CHAPTER 18

DON'T DRIFT

A ship that is sitting idle is not making money and not achieving its purpose. It is important to keep the wind in the sails or the motor running so you are moving toward your objective. Going nowhere rarely satisfies anyone. There is an old nautical proverb that says, "Wind in the sail keeps a sailor happy." Why? Because the sailor knows they are on the way home. Or the sailor knows they are headed to a new and exciting port.

However, drifting is not always bad. Sometimes, there is a purpose for drifting, but it is not aimless. Currents can be used to pull the ship along. There may be a time schedule involved—the docking site may not be available for a couple of days, so it is necessary to drift (not wasting fuel) till the timing is right.

Have a clear purpose, and do not drift. Many people throw themselves into their work or careers. Often, people are defined by what they do for a living. That is fine, but why are you working? Do you enjoy what you do? Do you enjoy the people with whom you work? Do you get to bring home a paycheck to the ones you love? It is extremely important to know your purpose in life.

From a Christian perspective, the purpose of life is to glorify God and carry out His commandments. Of course, it is possible to glorify God by working hard at your job and being an example to your coworkers. We must, however, keep moving forward in our faith.

Drifting in our faith is one of the most dangerous things in the life of a believer. I am convinced that contentment with our relationship with the Lord is a snare the enemy uses to derail a believer. I have said to my church often that contentment leads to complacency, which leads to carelessness, which leads to catastrophe. I have followed that up with "If our faith is not growing, it is shrinking." There is no such thing as stagnant faith. A boat adrift is a stagnant boat. A stagnant boat is an ineffective boat.

Purpose in your walk with Christ to never drift. Seek to know the Lord more and more. It takes time, effort, and sacrifice, but it is worth it. Keep His wind in your sails and be carried along by His Spirit. Jonah was a man who allowed Himself to drift. His life teaches us some great lessons on how to stay the course. The course we are called to as believers is to be on mission, even if the seas are not to our liking, we are to stay the course.

In the great story *The Lord of the Rings*, Aragorn, son of Arathorn, is to be the next High King of Gondor. He is the last of the line of Isildur and is the centuries-long awaited king. Yet, he walks away from this destiny. He does almost everything he can to *not* step into this role. As fate would have it, everything happens around him to where he has no choice but to step into his role. Without him doing so, all Middle Earth would fall to Sauron, the evil dark lord.

Although the stakes are nowhere near as high in our lives as saving all the world from warrish death, we are still called according to His purpose and are called to a mission of mercy that saves lives. In Ephesians 2:10, Paul declares we all have a calling to do good works, we are all called on mission for the glory of Christ. Often, we ignore or reject our mission because we find ourselves too busy, too lazy, or too self-absorbed to be on mission. We tend to choose our own path, our own way, and our own desires over the Lord's.

In this, we reflect Jonah. Jonah's negative example can give us some positive application on staying the course, however. I believe in this portion of Jonah's story, he answers the question, How can we embrace the Lord's mission of mercy?

STUDY FIRST

2 Kings 14:25; Jonah 1

Jonah was a proven prophet. The Lord came to him and gave him an unlikely and uncomfortable mission of unexpected and unwanted mercy. From Jonah's life, we are given six keys to embracing the Lord's mission.

KEY #1: THE LORD'S MISSION AND MERCY RARELY MAKE SENSE TO THE HUMAN MIND (2 KINGS 14:25; JONAH 1:1-2)

So much about this mission seemed off. For one, prophets from the Lord were never called to preach to the Gentile nations but simply to their own people, the Israelites. Jonah's call to the Gentiles is the first.

Second, Jonah himself would *not* be the prophet to choose for such a mission. His message mentioned in 2 Kings was one that was highly pro-Israel. While the other prophets were calling out the sin, Jonah was given the job to bring national encouragement.

Keller states, "The original readers of the book of Jonah would have remembered him as intensely patriotic, a highly partisan nationalist. And they would have been amazed that God would send a man like that to preach to the very people he most feared and hated."[59]

The Lord using Jonah reminds me that the Lord uses unlikely people for unlikely missions with undeserved mercy. Choosing both the Ninevites and Jonah was purposeful, although nonsensical (to our minds). Jonah knew that the Lord would only send him to pronounce judgment on the Ninevites if he was going to offer mercy. To Jonah, this did not make sense. How often do we see God's work in our lives or the lives of others and reject it because it doesn't make sense. Who are we to argue with the Lord?

KEY #2: OBEY THE LORD WHEN IT'S HARD, NOT JUST WHEN IT'S EASY (2 KINGS 14:25; JONAH 1:3)

When Jonah was preaching good things over Israel, obeying the Lord's direction was easy. Going into the land of his enemy was hard, so he fled. We always think of prophets as men who smiled in the face of adversity and always did the hard thing, but not Jonah.

---

59 Timothy Keller, *Rediscovering Jonah: The Secret of God's Mercy* (New York City: Penguin Publishing Group, 2020), 12. Kindle Edition.

Once the call became uncomfortable and he feared the Lord's mercy extended beyond his own, he ran away. To embrace the Lord's mission of mercy, we have to plunge headlong into obeying His voice despite the circumstances in which we are stepping. The Lord has a missionary heart, desiring all people hear about Him and have the merciful opportunity to turn to Him. Will we obey, even when it is hard to go?

For Jonah, this was hard on two fronts—he feared the people he was called to serve, and he feared the Lord would provide mercy to those whom he hated. The Ninevites were violent, cruel people who hated the Jews and would most likely kill Jonah if he delivered this message.

He also feared that the Lord would provide mercy in this message, and he wanted none of that, thinking he knew better than the Lord. Jonah was allowing his bias to hinder his obedience. Wiersbe says: "He not only hated their sins—and the Assyrians were ruthless enemies—but he hated the sinners who committed the sins."[60] Don't be like Jonah!

KEY #3: REFUSAL TO GO ON MISSION HINDERS OUR CONNECTION TO THE LORD (JONAH 1:3B)

An old preacher once said, "With the Lord, to disobey is to turn away." And it is so true. Jonah was disobedient to his mission, and he realized he had to turn away from the Lord to do so. He "arose" as the Lord had said, but in his "rising," he turned his back not only on the mission but also on the Lord Himself!

I love how Wiersbe puts it: "Jonah knew that he couldn't run away from God's presence (Psalm 139:7-12), but he felt he had the right to turn in his resignation."[61] Jonah knew his intimacy with the Lord would be affected. His connection to the voice of the Lord would be hindered. Yet his two fears were so great that he was willing to turn his back on the Lord.

---

60 Warren Wiersbe, *Be Amazed (Minor Prophets): Restoring an Attitude of Wonder and Worship*, (New York City: Victor Books, 2010), 73.
61 Ibid.

"God was no longer speaking to Jonah through His word; He was speaking to him through His works: the sea, the wind, the rain, the thunder, and even the great fish. Everything in nature obeyed God except His servant! God even spoke to Jonah through the heathen sailors"[62]

KEY #4: STORMS ARE DIFFICULTIES IN LIFE THAT CAN ARISE FROM THE SIN OF DISOBEDIENCE (JONAH 1:4-6)

Keller says, "The Bible does not say that every difficulty is the result of sin—but it does teach that every sin will bring you into difficulty."[63] Some sort of storm will result from our sin. Like in the story of Moses and his sin, our sin will always be found out.

I am not sure if Jonah anticipated such a dramatic and literal storm because of his sin, but we soon see that he realizes why it is there. We, too, will see storms arise in our lives due to our disobedience. Some storms may be small, and others may be large. We can learn from the storms in our lives. We can seek to learn from them rather than run from them. We can ask the Lord to use our storms for good rather than allowing them to destroy us.

Storms can sometimes mercifully redirect us back to obedience. Keller once said, "Storms can wake us up to truths we would otherwise never see. Storms can develop faith, hope, love, patience, humility, and self-control in us that nothing else can. And innumerable people have testified that they found faith in Christ and eternal life only because some great storm drove them toward God."[64]

KEY #5: REPENTANCE CAN HELP STILL THE STORMS STARTED BY OUR OWN SINS (JONAH 1:7-15)

This moment in Jonah's life is fascinating. He knows what he has done. The Lord knows what he has done. And now, the sailors know the full story

---

62 Wiersbe, 74.
63 Keller, 24.
64 Ibid, 28-29.

132 THE ANCHORED LIFE

of what he has done. They look to Jonah for a solution, and he only offers his own death.

B.K. Smith states, "He did not exhibit repentance for fleeing from the Lord but merely resigned himself to the only seeming solution."[65] When Jonah could have chosen repentance, he chose resignation. His sin was now not only affecting himself, but also these innocent sailors. He did not want them to die on his account, but his stubbornness to repent led him to only one solution—he must go.

This seems ludicrous, does it not? Wiersbe observes, "Jonah offered to die because selfishly he would rather die than obey the will of God."[66] Jonah so badly did not want to go to the Ninevites that he was willing to die in his stubbornness. There was no promise or hope of rescue. He refused to repent.

I think Jonah knew that repenting would lead him to turning back. The same old preacher I heard also said, "With the Lord, to obey is to turn away from the wrong way." If he repented, Jonah would have to then do the task he did not want to do. This he refused to do.

How often do we do the same? We would rather any way out of our self-caused storms than repent. Choose repentance!

KEY #6: ALLOW GOD'S MERCY TO EMPOWER YOUR MISSION (JONAH 1:16-17)

These sailors recognized they had received mercy from the Lord of Israel. In their recognition of this mercy, they made vows and changed allegiance from their previous god to the God of Israel. His mercy changed their lives.

If only Jonah would have allowed the Lord's mercy to do the same. He had seen the Lord offer mercy for a fallen people. Israel should have never received the mercy the Lord offered. Yet they were given great mercy. As

---

65 B.K. Smith and F.S. Page, *Amos, Obadiah, Jonah*, Vol. 19B (Nashville: Broadman and Holman Publishers, 1995), 235-36.
66 Wiersbe, 75.

a witness to this, Jonah should have recognized himself as a partaker of that mercy and seen his flawed, sinful self as a recipient of mercy.

Fully grasping God's mercy on us should inspire us to be on mission. May we be a people who choose the mission of mercy we are called to and not allow ourselves to drift as Jonah did. May we step into obedience and seek to live our whole lives on mission for Jesus.

KEY TAKEAWAY PRINCIPLES

- Do not drift without purpose.
- Going nowhere rarely satisfies anyone.
- Keep focused and busy; do not be lazy.
- Continue to lean into your calling.

FURTHER STUDY

- "Whatever you do, work heartily, as for the Lord and not for men" (Col. 3:23).
- "A slack hand causes poverty, but the hand of the diligent makes rich" (Prov. 10:4).
- "The hand of the diligent will rule, while the slothful will be put to forced labor" (Prov. 12:24).

CHAPTER 19
MAINTAIN ACCURATE FINANCIAL ACCOUNTING

Nothing is free. Most voyages are made for a purpose. Usually, that purpose is a business decision. Christopher Columbus was looking for a quicker trade route (to make more money faster). Captain Bligh and the *Bounty* were looking for another quick and inexpensive food staple. Even explorers or the military have budgets that must be maintained. Pirates want their fair share of the booty.

Money is mentioned a lot in the Bible. Some people are obsessed with it, and it becomes a sinful distraction. Money does not have to be negative. It is essential when it comes to tithing and supporting churches.

Maintaining professional financial accounting helps to maintain a healthy view of money. It is important to avoid the many pitfalls that the love of money can bring. We should not devote our lives to gathering and accumulating more wealth like we see in the parable of the rich fool, who pulled down his barns to build bigger ones (Luke 12:16-21). We should not be greedy like the Pharisees (Matt. 23:25). We should be generous with money and willing to pay back anyone we have wronged like Zacchaeus was (Luke 19:1-10). Finally, we should not only use but also grow our money and gifts for the glory of God like the master who entrusted talents to his servants in the parable of the talents (Matt. 25:14-30).

Looking closely at Zacchaeus, we see a man who loved money, power, and prestige to the detriment of his own people. He was a ruthless cheat; and it not only helped Rome (and his own bank account), but it also hindered his people. When Jesus invited Himself to the home of Zacchaeus, many were offended that he chose to dine with such a man.

Another greedy man in the life of Jesus was Judas Iscariot. Judas oversaw the money that came in for the disciples, and we know from Scripture that he was more than happy to help himself to the funds because he was a thief.[67]

Paul says to Timothy, "For the love of money is a root of all kinds of evils" (1 Tim. 6:10). Money is needed for mission, but money cannot become the mission. Having a distant relationship with money and seeing it as a tool is healthy. It is when we begin to be enamored by money and the "more" it can get us that we fall into an unhealthy love relationship with a dangerous bed partner.

We must, like Zacchaeus eventually did, release our longing for more and more money and be people of generosity. We cannot be foolish with our money, for money is needed to remain healthy, alive and on mission, but we cannot hoard it all for ourselves either. Take time to read the account of Zacchaeus in Luke 19:1-10 and see how the Lord's presence in his life changed his love for money into love for the mission.

KEY TAKEAWAY PRINCIPLES

- You must be accountable for your finances.
- Make sure there is an accurate accounting of such items as petty cash, salaries, bonuses, and fair share of cargo.
- Make sure investors (and God) are satisfied with their cut and return on investment.

FURTHER STUDY

- "'For it will be like a man going on a journey, who called his servants and entrusted to them his property. To one he gave five talents, to another two, to another one, to each according to his ability. Then he went away. He who had received the five talents

---

[67] John 12:4-6

went at once and traded with them, and he made five talents more. So also he who had the two talents made two talents more. But he who had received the one talent went and dug in the ground and hid his master's money'" (Matt. 25:14-18).

- "The point is this: whoever sows sparingly will also reap sparingly, and whoever sows bountifully will also reap bountifully. Each one must give as he has decided in his heart, not reluctantly or under compulsion, for God loves a cheerful giver. And God is able to make all grace abound to you, so that having all sufficiency in all things at all times, you may abound in every good work" (2 Cor. 9:6-8).

- "For because of this you also pay taxes, for the authorities are ministers of God, attending to this very thing. Pay to all what is owed to them: taxes to whom taxes are owed, revenue to whom revenue is owed, respect to whom respect is owed, honor to whom honor is owed" (Rom. 13:6-7).

CHAPTER 20

MAN OVERBOARD

You do not want to lose anyone on your journey. In life, when a dangerous crisis happens, it has to be dealt with immediately. Key employees dying, going on maternity leave, and leaving the company for better opportunities are all common issues for which you should anticipate and prepared.

Shouting, "Man overboard" is not just a statement to tell passengers you lost someone. It actually starts a process. There are three main steps in the process:

- Point at the person/victim.
- Keep your eye on the target.
- Yell, "Man overboard."

This is the beginning of the rescue process. Does the average person really do this? No. Do sailors who have been properly trained do this? Yes.

In the corporate world, everyone is familiar with the "Double P," otherwise known as Policies and Procedures. Sometimes, these are incorporated into a company manual or policy manual. Policies are quickly defined as rules and procedures that are the steps or procedures to be implemented.

On one of my (Tim) trips, the ship's beloved cat was accidentally blown off the deck and into the water. Multiple passengers followed the procedures. Several passengers even threw life preservers. The cat actually made it to one of the life preservers and hung on for dear life.

The captain took this opportunity to test and train his crew. He sounded the alarm. The full procedure went into action! The sails were lowered. The motorized launch was lowered into the water with a rescue and medical team on board. In record-breaking time, the launch made it to the exhausted feline. The captain sacrificed his schedule and possibly risked his crew to save a cat. However, this sacrifice made his crew greater as a team and more skilled at rescue procedures. The cat, after all, was a crew member!

In our Christian walk, we are to strive to walk alongside our Christian siblings and help them *not* go overboard or help someone get back on the boat after they have gone overboard. I (Marv) think this translates to "we need to be Samwise Gamgee to our brothers and sisters."

Let me explain. I have recently been rewatching *The Lord of the Rings*, and in doing so, one cannot escape being in utter awe of the little hobbit known as Samwise Gamgee. He is a deeply intriguing character because he seems to have nothing to gain in helping Frodo get to Mount Doom, yet he is the most stout-hearted and loyal person in the whole series. His is a love not often seen anymore—a love and affection of deep friendship. He follows Frodo to Mordor, but he also saves him from many dangers, even from himself in the end. He is loyal, but honest as well. Frodo even realizes in the end that he would be nothing without his loyal and trusting companion Samwise Gamgee. We need more Sams in this world, and we need to be more like Sam.

In the Scriptures, there is a story, a beautiful narrative of faith of a man just like Sam, named Jonathan. As we seek to better understand his narrative, I think we will find ourselves within his story, and we will see qualities of friendship that must once again prevail in our lives.

Too often, we do not realize our need for true, godly friendship. Friendship is much more important than we would let on, and too many of us are content to try and walk this difficult road of life alone or with "buddies" and not true Sam/Jonathan-like friendships. How do we find or be a Jonathan to help prevent a man from going overboard or to help one who already is overboard?

STUDY FIRST

Read 1 Samuel 18:1-5.

This portion of Jonathan's story gives great insight as to how he was as a friend and how much this friendship meant to him. Below, I will point out several lessons we can learn and how they apply to not letting a man go (or stay) overboard!

TRUE AND GODLY FRIENDS LOVE DEEPLY AND LIVE FAITHFULLY (1 SAM. 18: 1, 3)

After David defeated Goliath and Saul talked with David, Jonathan saw David was a man like him, one he could trust and love with the intimate relationship of a deep friendship. This love was no mere fleeting affection. It was deeply rooted enough to say that their "souls were knit together." It was rich, real, and raw. With his valiant defeat over a giant, David inspired Jonathan to see him as a hero; but he also saw David's need for a true friend who would deeply love him for who he was, not just what he could do, and he knew that David would be a man who would do the same. It is as C.S. Lewis said in *Surprised by Joy*: "Nothing, I suspect, is more astonishing in any man's life than the discovery that there do exist people very, very like himself."[68]

As a prince, it was hard for Jonathan to find someone enough like him with whom he could share a bond of true friendship. Everyone was out to "love him," and yet no one was there to love him at all. Here, we see Saul loving David and Jonathan realizing he has a friend because of it. Jonathan chooses to love, and we will see how this love will change his life.

True and godly friendship is both honest and safe. In our lives, we tend to build walls against people. We do not let people in too closely. We do not confess our sins, walk closely, or share our fears and doubts with others often. Nor do others feel safe doing so with us. This is a sad loss for the Church. For

---

68   C.S. Lewis, *Surprised by Joy: The Shape of My Early Life* (San Francisco: HarperOne, 2017), 46.

when we live this way, we do not have true community. There is no real sense of love within such relationships.

In today's world, it is easy to put up walls and choose not to actually love. "We can choose not to love and have a heart of stone,[sic] it will never get hurt but it will never be joyful either. Or we can choose to love and experience both the joy of love and the pain of heartbreak. One is death,[sic] the other is life. I choose life."[69]

Jonathan also chose life, as did David. True and godly friendship is reciprocal. Our hearts long for this type of true, godly friendship; yet sadly, we do not find it often in the church. We must first *be* true and godly friends. The more of us who choose to *be* this type of friend will find the more readily we can find friends like this. In loving and being safe, we reflect the Lord. Only through the Spirit's power can we be loving, safe friends!

TRUE AND GODLY FRIENDS ARE GENEROUS AND SACRIFICIAL (1 SAM. 18:2-4; JOHN 15:13)

Love is also not a fleeting emotional response to another person. Love, as the great band DC Talk said, is a verb. There is action to love, not just emotion or sentiment. Here, we see an immediate response from Jonathan. He takes off his royal robe and places it on David.

One commentator says, "The fact that Jonathan gave David the garb and armaments originally reserved for the heir to Saul's throne clearly possesses symbolic and thematic significance."[70] In essence, he is saying, "I love you so much, I recognize that *you* are to be the next king, not me. I love you and God so much that I will let this happen; and in fact, I will help you bear it." Love is sacrificial. Here, Jonathan symbolically gives up his right to his throne because he recognizes David to be the next king, and he is okay with it.

---

69 C.S. Lewis, *The Four Loves: The Much Beloved Exploration of the Nature of Love* (San Francisco: HarperOne, 2017), 20.
70 R.D. Bergen, *1, 2 Samuel, Vol. 7* (Nashville: Broadman & Holman Publishers, 1996).

Samwise gave up the shire; Jonathan gave up his throne; and in this deep world of necessary friendship love, each of us will have to give up something as well. Here again, we see our culture creeping into this. It is hard to sacrifice and hard to give things up; and the world around us says we must not. We need to keep all we get.

According to the world, to give up something like a throne or your comfort is folly. Yet we see that in order to do great things, sacrifices must be made. In order for David to be king, he needed Jonathan's sacrifice. In order to actually throw the ring into the volcano, Frodo needed Samwise's sacrifice to go with him. Look at all the great stories in history, and we will notice a common thread of loving friends giving up something so the main protagonist could save the day. Jesus, our best Friend, gave his life so that we could be saved. This love is laced throughout every narrative; it permeates history; and it is a needed piece of our lives. Do you have friends you love so deeply?

TRUE AND GODLY FRIENDS SEE AND THEN CALL OUT THE BEST IN ONE ANOTHER (1 SAM. 18:4)

Jonathan saw the Lord in David. Jonathan saw the king David would become, and he spoke it into David's future. Jonathan abdicated his right to the throne and gave it to David because Jonathan knew the Lord had called David and not himself. We have got to be people who speak the love of Jesus into friends and call the best of Jesus out of friends!

TRUE AND GODLY FRIENDS CALL EACH OTHER OUT (1 SAM. 20:1-4)

Here, in another portion of the story of David and Jonathan, we see David suggesting something and Jonathan disagreeing with him. Jonathan was not afraid to get in David's face a little bit, saying that his father would never plan to kill David without first consulting with himself. They then work out a plan to see if David is safe or not. The point here is that Jonathan was not afraid to be real about his feelings and issues.

This may seem like a very hard pull from the text, but I guarantee it is not. This is a feud that could have ended less stable friendships. David accuses his friend's father of plotting a murder! That is some big stuff. Jonathan is not afraid to deny this strongly but is also willing to check it out. He gets in his face but does not walk away from him.

Proverbs 27:6 says, "Faithful are the wounds of a friend; profuse are the kisses of an enemy." This means that when a friend—someone you know loves you and whom you also love with the deep, rich, real love—gets in your face, you can trust that wound. It may hurt, but it may help as well.

It is really easy to blockade oneself from friends who can be real with us. We do not want to hear it, so we have buddies instead of true friends—people who will only whisper the nice things about us and hold back the negative. We also are buddies to others by simply staying away from wounding anyone. That is not love. Love desires the best for their friends. So, a true friend is honest. They listen to the deepest, darkest portions of one's soul, and then they offer a loving rebuke when needed.

We need more of this in our lives. It will be difficult to accept the rebukes of our friends, but they love us and only desire our growth. I need someone to get into my face, and I know you probably do, too. Let us choose love. It is vulnerable, and it will hurt. But we cannot do great things without it, and God chose sacrificial love and chose a get-in-your-face love for us. Let us seek to find a Jonathan and be a Jonathan so the world can know us by our love!

TRUE AND GODLY FRIENDS MAKE SURE TO HAVE EACH OTHER'S BACKS (1 SAM. 20:33, 42)

Jonathan made a promise to David that he would protect him. Although they disagreed, Jonathan sought to find out the truth of the matter as to whether Saul really wanted to kill David or not. Jonathan quickly found out and not only stood up to Saul, but also protected David from certain death as well.

A true and godly friend defends you. A true and godly friend is in your corner. A true and godly friend lets you know what people are saying about you and informs you if someone is out to harm you. A true and godly friend is not afraid to stand by your side when it seems everyone is against you. We need those friends. We also need to *be* those friends!

In reflecting on Jonathan and David, Alan Redpath asks his readers, "Would you ask the Holy Spirit to make you a friend like that and to . . . cultivate within your life friendships like this?"[71] I ask you the same question. Will you be a true, godly friend? Will you seek out true, godly friendships?

We need to choose to love and pursue true, godly friendships! Let me share with you a powerful and challenging quote from C.S. Lewis:

> To love at all is to be vulnerable. Love anything and your heart will be wrung and possibly broken. If you want to make sure of keeping it intact you must give it to no one, not even an animal. Wrap it carefully round with hobbies and little luxuries; avoid all entanglements. Lock it up safe in the casket or coffin of your selfishness. But in that casket, safe, dark, motionless, airless, it will change. It will not be broken; it will become unbreakable, impenetrable, irredeemable.[72]

KEY TAKEAWAY PRINCIPLES

- It is important to follow these set procedures.
  - Point.
  - Eyes on target.
  - Throw a life preserver.
  - Yell, "Man overboard" (or "Cat overboard").
- Sometimes, you must focus on one person.

---

71 Alan Redpath, *The Making of a Man of God: Lessons from the Life of David* (Grand Rapids: Fleming H. Revell, 2004), 52.
72 C. S. Lewis, *The Four Loves*, 20.

THE ANCHORED LIFE

- Understand the importance of morale and training.
- Be observant. Looking and listening are important concepts.

FURTHER STUDY

- "Open my eyes, that I may behold wondrous things out of your law" (Psalm 119:18).
- "The hearing ear and the seeing eye, the LORD has made them both" (Prov. 20:12).
- "Turn my eyes from looking at worthless things; and give me life in your ways" (Psalm 119:37).
- "The eyes of the LORD are in every place, keeping watch on the evil and the good" (Prov. 15:3).

PART 4

LEADERSHIP PRINCIPLES: MANAGING THE CREW

Dealing with the crew or employees is almost always the most difficult part of being a leader. People are not machines. "Taskmaster" obviously has a negative connotation, but there are always task issues that must be handled. We immediately know the characteristics that go with this term. Obviously, you do not want to be a difficult boss, but it is important to maintain a strong work ethic and productivity without alienating your crew. It is important that good leaders try to be decisive, empathetic, accountable, ethical, and dependable. Good communication is critical to these traits.

I (Marv) want to pause and focus on one of my favorite leaders in the Bible—Nehemiah. His life teaches us well the idea of "managing the crew."

One of the things my wife and I are always reminding our oldest son is that he is a leader to his siblings. We often mention to him that they are watching him, what he does, what he says, how he reacts to correction, and how he respects us. Unfortunately for him, as the oldest, his life is on display to the other two. He has influence in their lives based on the simple fact that he is the oldest. He does not always like it, and his leadership of them is not always stellar, but he has begun to understand that he is leading them whether he wants to or not.

Similarly, we are all leaders. John Maxwell says, "Everyone is a leader because everyone influences someone."[73] As believers, fathers, mothers, workers, bosses, and so on, our lives are being watched, and we are leading

---

73 John C. Maxwell, *Developing the Leader Within You* (Nashville: Thomas Nelson, 2006), 21.

someone. It is no wonder, then, we are introduced to leaders in Scripture and are admonished to follow their examples.

Too often in leadership, we look to the world to teach us how to lead. Yet the Scriptures are full of leadership principles that we can put in place in our own lives. So, how can we become effective Christian leaders?

STUDY FIRST

Read Nehemiah 1:1-11; 2:1-8, 13, 17.

Nehemiah was the cupbearer to King Artaxerxes I, who held dominion over the people of Israel. We can assume Nehemiah's book occurred starting in 445 B.C. Nehemiah's story began in a humble, yet privileged way. Being the cupbearer to the king in that time was a high honor, yet he was unknown to his own people. This cupbearer would become an essential example of godly, Christian leadership.

In his book, Nehemiah shows us what a good leader should look like. His life offers us five principles for Christian leadership, and these principles matter to each and every one of us as followers of Christ.

LEADERS CARE ABOUT THEIR FOLLOWERS

Nehemiah took the time out of his life to ask how things were going in his home country. He was a cupbearer who was living in the luxury, pleasure, and leisure of the king. He did not need anything from the people of Israel, but he cared enough to ask how they were and how things were going. Warren Wiersbe says, "Why would Nehemiah inquire about a struggling remnant of people who lived hundreds of miles away? After all, he was the king's cupbearer and he was successfully secure in his own life."[74]

In Nehemiah, we see a man who cared about others. He set his own life aside and jumped in with his life to help his people rebuild the wall. Nehemiah

---

74 Warren W. Wiersbe, *Be Determined: Standing Firm in the Face of Opposition: OT Commentary: Nehemiah* (Colorado Springs: David C. Cook, 2009), 21.

did not need to ask about the people. He simply had a natural inclination toward caring about his people. As Wiersbe points out, Nehemiah's life was set. Nehemiah did not need anyone or anything, much less the need to worry about other people. If they were in a similar situation as Nehemiah, many people, left to themselves, would slough off the worry about other people and would live their lives in a manner unto themselves.

Selfish leadership is poor leadership. Selflessness is a great attribute of a good leader. If we do not care about our people and simply live our leadership life to get ahead for ourselves, we stop being a leader and start being a dictator.

Our early picture of Nehemiah shows the type of leader he would show himself to be: one who cared deeply for others. Gene Wilkes says, "As long as leaders are worried about who sits at the head table, they have little time for the people they are called to serve."[75] Nehemiah cared about Israel, their situation, and the situation of the Lord's city.

LEADERS PRAY BEFORE ANYTHING ELSE (NEH. 1:4).

Nehemiah does not simply care for people and leave it there; he goes before the almighty God on their behalf! When Nehemiah hears the devastating news, whether it is old news or new news to him, he is stricken with grief. His grief, however, leads him first to his knees. He does not just pray a simple prayer either! Nehemiah fasts and prays. He enters into the pain of his people. His care leads him to seek the only One Who can give the answers to the problem at hand.

What could Nehemiah do about the pain of his people? Nothing! So, he needs guidance from the Lord. This shows the heart of a leader who is willing to stand in the gap for his people!

If they believe in Jesus Christ, great leaders (spiritual or not) should be praying leaders. If we claim that Jesus is our "all in all" yet do not ask Him to

---

75 C. Gene Wilkes, *Jesus on Leadership* (Wheaton: Tyndale House Publishers, 1998), 36.

assist us and those we lead, we are simply giving lip service to a faith that has no bearing in our real life. By praying, Nehemiah was seeking the best for others, not himself. When we pray as leaders, we are seeking what God would have us do for Him and for His people, not ourselves.

When we lead in this way, we are acting as Jesus did in the capacity of a Servant-leader. Before we lead our families and our followers, or make any decisions at all, our first act should be to pray. Pray before we discipline our children. Pray before we make a change to our organization. Pray before we speak to an employee who messed up. Prayer needs to be our first response to any situation. Prayer gives us the guidance we need to lead well.

Nehemiah shows us that leaders turn to prayer first. He also shows us that our prayer is not just for guidance, but also specifically for those we lead.

LEADERS PRAY SPECIFICALLY FOR THEIR PEOPLE (NEH. 1:5-11)

Not only did Nehemiah care enough to say a simple prayer for his people, but like a priest, he also interceded for them before God. He went to the living God and asked Him for mercy upon the people. Leaders care enough to pray for their people in this way.

For leaders, this type of praying can go a long way with their leadership, not only because it trains them to become better prayers, but also because it helps them to be closer to the people they lead. There is always a need for a harsh word spoken in love, for sure, but there is also a time for tender intercession where we as leaders seek God's forgiveness of them.

While reading about the leadership of Nehemiah, I am struck with the reality that I rarely do this for my people. I am convicted by Nehemiah's example and desire to be a leader who intercedes for the people I lead!

Nehemiah was also claiming the promises from 1 Kings 8:29 and 2 Chronicles 7:14 that God would be attentive to the prayers of His people. Wiersbe says, "God's eyes are upon His people and His ears are open to their prayers (1 Kings 8:29; 2 Chronicles 7:14)."[76] The Lord hears our prayers. Let us pray for our children, our spouses, our coworkers, and those we lead in Sunday school. We should pray often for anyone under the influence of our leadership. Prayer is vital! Once we have prayed, we must then take the action the Lord leads us to take.

LEADERS WALK IN BOLDNESS, NOT FEAR (NEH. 2:1-8)

In these verses, we see Nehemiah listening to and acting on his prayers to God. In his time of prayer, the Lord clearly led him. Nehemiah boldly asks the king if he may go and rebuild the wall that had been destroyed in Jerusalem. Nehemiah asks his boss to give him paid time off for who knew how long. Not only does he ask to be relieved from his duty, but he also boldly asks the king to finance the renovation of the wall of his conquered people! He is essentially a high-ranking slave asking his master to let him go—and with tons of cash as he goes! But as Nehemiah says, "And the king granted me what I asked, for the good hand of my God was upon me" (Neh. 2:8b).

I believe because of Nehemiah's care and prayer, he was able to foresee that the king would grant his request. He could go boldly before the king because in his prayer, Nehemiah was certain of the outcome. God told him what it was, and he obeyed! Even during the discussion, Nehemiah prayed (Neh. 2:4). In his going, he was asking the Lord for continued boldness and favor. He was not relying upon himself, but on the Lord.

We can be bold because when we pray first and clearly hear the strategy from the Lord, we know He is with us! Where God guides, He provides!

LEADERS GIVE THOUGHTFUL GUIDANCE (NEH. 2:13, 17)

Nehemiah took the time to see what he needed to do before he did it. Good leaders take the time to assess the situation and do not just rush in and

---

76 Wiersbe, 19.

try to fix things. This is a lesson I need to learn. I sometimes rush into things without thinking and without assessing the situation. Generally, I have a good sense of what must be done, but I do not always have the steps to get there unless I sit down and assess the full picture. Too often in my life, I have rushed into things and have hindered the progress of getting things done.

Nehemiah did not make that mistake. He simply took time out to go and inspect the walls to see what needed to be done. He observed the places that needed extra care and the places that would be quick and easy to rebuild. Wiersbe says, "A good leader doesn't rush into his work but patiently gathers the facts firsthand and then plans his strategy" (Prov. 18:13). Nehemiah has taken the time to assess the situation, to care about the people, and to pray to ask God what must be done.

Finally, he is ready to cast the vision to the people and get them on board with the mission. His steps are deliberate and wise. He did not rush into telling them what must be done and how he was going to do it. He took the time to patiently seek the Lord and to patiently see what ought to be done and think through how best to get it done. He cast the vision, but not prematurely, in a way that rallied the people around the vision.

In our areas of leadership, be they small or large, we must follow the example of Nehemiah. When leading our families, nothing can stress out our spouses more than a rushed decision. Nothing can blow up in our faces faster than a thoughtless move. If we are to lead well, we need to slow down, assess the situation, hear the voice of the Lord, and then take action.

CHAPTER 21
CHAIN OF COMMAND

The chain of command is the official hierarchy of authority of who is in charge. The chain of command dictates who takes orders and who receives orders. You cannot have a seaman going to the admiral for orders. This hierarchy is essential in establishing clear responsibility in an organization. This was clearly established by Nehemiah in his efforts to lead the rebuilding of the wall. His enemies did not like the chain of command, but they could not do anything about it!

In the previous chapter, we looked at some principles of leadership from the life of Nehemiah on "managing the crew." We also saw some areas about the chain of command coming into play within the story of Nehemiah. In this chapter, we will conclude those thoughts on Nehemiah's leadership principles.

I remember it like it was yesterday. I was leading a mission trip to Paris, France. I had to make it to church on time, and it was not too far off the subway, so I figured I could get my team there, no problem. I was leading our team, and a college student from the church plant piped up, "I think you're taking us the wrong way."

I doubted his assertion, so we looked at a map. We could not understand the road signs properly, so, we had no idea if we were truly lost or not. We then tried to ask strangers (who only spoke French) where we were and how to get where we needed to go. This did not help until I pulled out my translating app. I had led my team on an expedition in the wrong direction. We were righted and made it to church on time. Sometimes, we think we are leading

154 THE ANCHORED LIFE

in the right direction when, in fact, we are not. Humility in leadership is vital to healthy leadership.

STUDY FIRST

Read Nehemiah 3:1-2; 4:7-9, 13-20; 6:2-3, 12-13; 12:27.

In his book, Nehemiah shows us what a good leader should look like. His life offers us several principles for Christian leadership, and these principles matter to each and every one of us as followers of Christ and especially to every leader.

LEADERS KNOW THEIR PEOPLE

Along with this idea of delegation, a leader must know who to place where. In Nehemiah 3, we see certain people doing certain jobs. Nehemiah must have known who would work best where, and so he placed them in their area of strength to get the job done to the best of their ability. This also means that Nehemiah knew the people well enough to put them in their areas of strength! He took the time to assess each individual to then place them where they needed to be.

This is a powerful lesson in leadership! If we are to be good leaders, we need to know the people we are leading so we can fit them into the role in which they can best work. Nehemiah made sure that each person he was leading had their specific role where they could shine and do their work well. Delegating is essential to healthy Christian leadership.

LEADERS DEAL WITH OPPOSITION (NEH. 4 AND 6)

When God uses people to do great things or when great things are done, there will almost always be opposition. To the enemies of the Israelites, the wall represented stability and safety, so when they saw great progress being made on the wall, they were angry (Neh. 4:7). They were going to mess up this progress that was happening in Jerusalem. It was not going to happen on their watch.

God often defies the desires of sinful men. Nehemiah knew how to handle this type of opposition, and he was ready for it. Once he saw what the enemies of Jerusalem were plotting, he gathered people together to pray. As a leader, he knew he was also a follower of God. He knew his role and sought God for advice. God had asked him to build the wall, so God must have had a plan to protect the wall from being destroyed again.

After praying, Nehemiah came up with a battle plan—set a guard day and night as protection (Neh. 4:9). He also set up people ready to fight, and we hear that this frustrated the plans of their enemies (Neh. 4:15). This battle plan stopped their enemies in their tracks, because the Jews were ready to fight when their enemies expected them to be vulnerable while building the wall.

Leaders lead with both a hammer and a sword (Neh. 4:17). Nehemiah did not rest assured with just frustrating their plans; he also ensured the safety of his people. Once opposition came and left, he was not under the delusion that it would not pop up again. In fact, he readied his people for it to happen at any moment. He prepared them with weapons as well as a plan of action if more opposition were to creep up on them.

Nehemiah prepared his people for more trouble, and this preparing of his people is a great principle for leadership! Christian leaders train their people to both build and protect. When we stop training our people to build and protect, we become vulnerable to the enemy's attacks. Satan is a lion, waiting for his prey (1 Peter 5:8), and God's people need to know how to have a hammer (to do the work of God) in one hand and a sword (to fight off the enemy) in the other. Opposition will come. Leaders need to deal with it and train their followers to do the same.

LEADERS ARE DISCERNING (NEH. 6)

Who is really in charge when it comes to Christian leadership? Who is at the top of the chain of command? The answer is Christ. So, we must discern His will.

Nehemiah was not fooled by the tricks of the enemy. They began offering help to rebuild, instead of opposing progress. Most leaders may have been excited to see the new change in the opposition, but not Nehemiah. Nehemiah discerned that their true and ultimate intention was to harm him, not to help him. I enjoy what Warren Wiersbe says, "Leaders must take care that they cooperate with the right people at the right time for the right purpose; otherwise, they may end up cooperating with the enemy. Satan is a master deceiver and has his servants ready to join hands with God's people so he can weaken their hands in the work (2 Corinthians 11:13-15)."[77]

Who we partner with matters. Although these old enemies were playing nice now, Nehemiah could tell that they would soon become his enemies again after they "helped" rebuild the wall.

Nehemiah was a discerning leader in more than one instance. Here we see him perceiving the one who prophesied was actually sent by the enemy (Neh. 6:12). He saw that this man was not sent by God and that his words were false. Leaders need to know which people to listen to because it could spell disaster for us in the future if we listen to the wrong people.

I think the illustration of counterfeit money comes into play here. The police in charge of detecting counterfeit money study the real money closely. They spend time learning it, understanding it, and gaining a deep-rooted understanding of the real thing.

When we spend intimate time with the Lord and get to hear His heartbeat and allow His Spirit to speak deeply into our lives, we, like Nehemiah, will be able to very quickly determine or discern that which is fake. Nehemiah's intimacy with the Lord was directly connected to his intimacy with the Word of God. Warren Wiersbe says, "Nehemiah knew that Shemaiah was a false prophet because the message he delivered was contradictory to the Word of God."[78] Discernment in leadership keeps us on the right path.

---

77 Wiersbe, 84.
78 Ibid, 76.

LEADERS REMEMBER GOD'S GOODNESS (NEH. 9)

Nehemiah 9 is all about repenting and remembering the goodness of God. After rediscovering the Word of God in Nehemiah 8, the people realize their own sin and the goodness of their God. The Law spoke so deeply to their hearts that they realized just how sinful they had become, and they had no more reason to be confused about God seeming to have abandoned them—which, of course, He had not. He simply removed his blessing and allowed them to become captured.

All of this—the reading of the Law and the repenting—were led by Nehemiah. Nehemiah was a man who knew his faults and sins and realized his complete and utter dependence upon the Lord. The entire book is filled with Nehemiah confessing his dependence upon God and how it was God Who did all the work.

Leaders confess their inability and declare God's ability. We cannot claim our gifts. We had no choice in the matter. God chose those gifts, and the Holy Spirit delivered them. Nehemiah recognized this, and his example caused the entire nation to confess their own sin and, in turn, remember the goodness of God by recounting aloud His wonderful works. God is good!

LEADERS ARE TO BE THE ONES WHO GO FIRST (NEH. 10)

After repenting and remembering the goodness of God, the leaders decided that they were going to make a covenant to follow the Law. This they would declare to the people of Jerusalem and sign a document in front of them, all proving the seriousness in what they were about to undertake. Seeing the severity of their sins and the great goodness of God convicted them to change their lives, and the leaders decided to go first.

The great thing I notice in chapter ten is that at the top of the list is Nehemiah. He signed the document first! This may seem like a small principle of leadership or a small gesture by Nehemiah, but I think it speaks volumes.

Leaders who call for change, whether radical or not, must be willing to make the change first and, like Nehemiah, sign the covenant of change before anyone else does. Leaders do not ask their people to go somewhere they are not willing to go themselves.

LEADERS SEEK TO CELEBRATE WINS (NEH. 12)

Leaders need to show emotion when things go right. There must be a celebration when we come to the completion of a project and see what the Lord has done. It is really cool to see the excitement that Nehemiah and the people have at the end when the wall is successfully rebuilt. Not only was the wall built, but God also changed the hearts of the people through the building of the wall. That is something worth celebrating! I believe that we as leaders need to be more positive and find real wins where and when we can and then celebrate them.

Christian leadership requires a lot, but everything we need is available from the Lord, as we see from Nehemiah's life. Delegation, dealing well with opposition, discernment, remembrance of God's goodness, going first, and celebrating wins are not just good leadership practices, they are also Christian leadership practices. Let us resolve to put them in place.

KEY TAKEAWAY PRINCIPLE

- Know who your boss is.
- Do not violate the chain of command.
- There may be consequences if you violate the hierarchy.

STUDY FURTHER

- "Let every person be subject to the governing authorities. For there is no authority except from God, and those that exist have been instituted by God" (Rom. 13:1).

- "Obey your leaders and submit to them, for they are keeping watch over your souls, as those who will have to give an account. Let them do this with joy and not with groaning, for that would be of no advantage to you" (Heb. 13:17).
- "So that at the name of Jesus every knee should bow, in heaven and on earth and under the earth, and every tongue confess that Jesus Christ is Lord, to the glory of God the Father" (Phil. 2:10-11).

CHAPTER 22
DON'T DO IT ALONE

There is too much work to be done by any single person. Moses could not do it alone; Nehemiah could not do it alone; and Jesus *chose* not to do it alone! Leaders need to remember that they have to delegate tasks and assignments. The key elements of delegation are responsibility, authority, and accountability.

Micromanaging is a term that is often used to describe a management style where the manager closely controls their subordinates. It is generally considered a negative term because the employee is not trusted or allowed workplace freedom. Delegating duties gives other people the opportunity to learn and grow. When extra responsibilities are given to individuals, it shows they can be trusted and are respected.

In general, I believe it is best to automatically lead from a place of trust. Those I lead have my trust, and it is up to them to keep it or lose it. Some leadership styles start from a place of distrust and demand their subordinates earn their trust. I feel this is a dangerous and toxic approach. Jesus sent out His disciples alone after having them with him for a period of time. He trusted them, instructed them, and then debriefed them afterward.

STUDY FIRST
Read 1 Timothy 1-3.

Any good captain is going to try to develop his crew, so he can know them enough to trust them. Not going it alone on the voyage of life includes discipleship and raising others up to not only work alongside you but also to one day replace you.

Paul was a master at this, especially with three younger men: Timothy, Titus, and Philemon. Paul was close with these three men, but Scripture speaks more to Paul's deep relationship with Timothy. Paul knew Timothy's mother and grandmother. Timothy was half Jew, and half Gentile. Yet despite Timothy's less-than-perfect ethnical makeup, Paul paid close attention to Timothy.

We see Paul mention Timothy often in his letters and then Paul entrusts Timothy with the task of helping the fledgling church in Ephesus. Paul writes 1 and 2 Timothy while Timothy is in Ephesus. Paul was in Ephesus a long period of time but raised up Timothy to do the ministry with him there and, eventually, to take over.

We can know that Paul truly *knew* Timothy, not only because of the family commentary that Paul speaks of but also because of how he addressed Timothy in his letters. In the opening of his first recorded letter to Timothy, he states, "To Timothy, my true child in the faith" (1 Tim. 1:2). The word "child" used here is τέκνον in Greek, and it does mean child, or son, but it also can mean "descendants from a common ancestor."[79] I think this idea of child—but also descendant—is important to the relationship of Paul and Timothy. He is essentially saying with this word (throughout the book of 1 Timothy), "You will be the pastor who takes the lead when I am gone." He is seeing Timothy more or less as his replacement when he dies.

Paul *knew* Timothy, and so he tailored his letter to Timothy in order to properly *equip* Timothy. Throughout the letters of 1 and 2 Timothy, Paul fills the pages with equipping language. He outlines the needs of the church, since Paul himself spent significant time there, and then walks Timothy through the ways needed to handle such a church.

Part of this equipping fits directly into the idea of giving influence. Paul's letters were always read aloud to the church. Gordon Fee states, "Paul is writing to Timothy with the full expectation that the church in Ephesus

---

[79] W. Arndt, F.W. Danker, W. Bauer, and F.W. Gingrich, F. W. *A Greek-English Lexicon of the New Testament and Other Early Christian Literature*, 3rd ed., s.v. τέκνον (Chicago: University of Chicago Press, 2000), 994.

will overhear. The errors being spread in the church call for Timothy's strong action, action ultimately based on Paul's apostolic authority."[80]

Paul is using his own authority here to bestow authority on Timothy. This is affirmed in Paul's statement in 1 Timothy 1:18: "This charge I entrust to you, Timothy, my child." Essentially, he is saying for all to hear, "By my authority, I give you authority." Paul continues, "In accordance with the prophecies previously made about you," stating to the church in Ephesus that "God has called Timothy to this through prophetic words!"

Paul is not only giving authority and influence but also teaching Timothy how to use it. He also reminds Timothy of what may have been the most powerful time in the young pastor's life, "Do not neglect the gift you have, which was given you by prophecy when the council of elders laid their hands on you" (1 Tim. 1:14).

He also gives a strong word of encouragement to Timothy (and a rebuke to the church in Ephesus) when he states, "Let no one despise you for your youth, but set the believers an example in speech, in conduct, in love, in faith, in purity" (1 Tim. 4:12). Gordon Fee comments:

> It is first of all a word of encouragement to Timothy, because he was in fact a younger man (thirty to thirty-five)—and perhaps timid (cf. 1 Cor. 16:10-11; 2 Tim. 1:6ff.). In a culture where "elders" were highly regarded, and in a church where the elders would have been older than he, this is not an insignificant encouragement. But for the same reasons, it is likewise a word to the community, to let them know that, despite his youth, he has Paul's own authority to command and teach these things (v. 11).[81]

The idea of *releasing* is also all throughout the entirety of the letters to Timothy, Titus, and Philemon. Essentially, these men had already been *released* into ministry of leading churches. Helping them in their positions is the impetus for Paul's letters. Each church had its own issues, and Paul, knowing

---

80 G.D. Fee, *1 and 2 Timothy, Titus* (Ada: Baker Books, 2011).
81 Ibid, 106-7.

those issues, wrote his letters of encouragement and instruction. Paul had trained these men, walked with these men, knew these me, equipped these men, and then released these men.

The issue of raising up the next generation of leaders, empowering them for ministry is all throughout Scripture. Jesus and Paul are a small New Testament microcosm of this macrocosmic biblical value. Some would argue that this type of empowerment is and should be the proper way of discipling, as I do. If we are to embark on a voyage on the sea of life, we need to learn how to know, equip, and release those around us. Otherwise, we will try to steer a large ship all by ourselves. Some leaders like that, but it always causes a crash at sea when they do!

KEY TAKEAWAY PRINCIPLES

- Do not be a micromanager.
- Understand the value of teams, communities, and departments.
- Know when to trust your subordinates.
- Disciple well. Disciple often.

STUDY FURTHER

- "Therefore encourage one another and build one another up, just as you are doing" (1 Thess. 5:11).
- "Two are better than one, because they have a good reward for their toil. For if they fall, one will lift up his fellow. But woe to him who is alone when he falls and has not another to lift him up! Again, if two lie together, they keep warm, but how can one keep warm alone? And though a man might prevail against one who is alone, two will withstand him—a threefold cord is not quickly broken" (Eccl. 4:9-12).

CHAPTER 23
TRAIN THE CREW

A highly trained crew can move quicker and safer to get the job done. An ineffective, unexperienced crew can be slow and possibly endanger themselves or the ship. It is important that officers and crew alike are constantly training and bettering themselves. Opportunities for education and training should be constantly available. Employees with more experience and education are usually more confident and create a better workplace environment.

Jesus lived life with the twelve disciples and was training them the entire time they were together. They traveled together, ate together, stayed in homes together, worshipped together, laughed together, learned together, and wept together. One of the many ways Jesus discipled and trained the twelve was through asking good questions and telling parables. Jesus was a master at asking questions. In counting the questions Jesus asks in the gospels, we can see he asked 307 recorded questions. Jesus' questions were both deep and penetrating. In the Gospel of John, we see quite quickly Jesus' approach of discipleship through asking questions. He asks, "'What are you seeking?'" (John 1:38).

In Matthew 16:13-15, Jesus asks two questions: "'Who do people say that the Son of Man is?'" and "'Who do you say that I am?'" These penetrating questions forced the disciples to think long and hard. We know Peter then proclaimed Who Christ is with great gusto. In this, so much about Peter (and the other disciples) was exposed.

Good questions help to train your crew. Giving certain scenarios on the "seas of life" through questions helps them think through navigating that terrain before it even appears.

166 THE ANCHORED LIFE

Jesus was leading and growing these men through the rabbinical form of teaching through questions. These questions not only served as tools for discipleship and training, but also as an avenue to *know* His disciples. Edgar Shein says, "The kind of inquiry I am talking about derives from an attitude of interest and curiosity. It implies a desire to build a relationship that will lead to more open communication."[82] This type of knowing is a very important part of training the young leaders of today; without it, you will have little voice into those who follow your command.

Jesus' close, life-on-life relationship with these twelve men gave Him not only a window into their lives but also the ability to speak into their lives. He knew them, their families, their needs, their fears, their struggles, and the areas in which they needed to grow. Jesus *knew* these men. Through Jesus's knowing, He was then able to equip His disciples.

The questions Jesus asked and the parables Jesus told allowed Jesus and the disciples themselves to see the areas of need and weakness within the disciples. Jesus asked these questions all throughout Scripture, and it exposed areas of needed growth in those of whom he asked questions.

My favorite example has to be in John 5, where Jesus heals a man at the pool of Bethesda. Jesus was in Jerusalem, and He stopped by a pool that was believed to have healing powers. It was said that when the water would stir, an angel of God was doing the stirring. The first person to get into the stirring pool would be healed. It is no surprise, then, that many lame, blind, and paralyzed men and women would be there, waiting for the water to stir, so they could be healed. Jesus came to this pool and found one man who had been there for thirty-eight years, and He asked him a simple question: "'Do you want to be healed?'" (John 5:6).

This question must have seemed foolish to those around Jesus. This man had been here for thirty-eight years, hoping to get into the water and receive

---

82 Edgar Shein, *Humble Inquiry: The Gentle Art of Asking Instead of Telling*, (Oakland: Berrett-Koehler Publishers, 2013), 19.

his healing. He desired freedom for his paralytic state, so why would Jesus ask such a silly question? I think it is because Jesus was exposing a hidden secret in this man's heart—contentment in his plight.

This man's whole life was wrapped up in his plight. His "job" was begging, and if he were to be healed now, his whole life would change. The life expectancy for many in Jesus's time was around forty years old. That means that this man was simply waiting it out. He was satisfied with where he was because it was what he was known for his whole life. Do not be too quick to judge this man either. We can tend to remain caged as well because we are content with the view.

Fear of the unknown can block us from freedom. Warren Wiersbe says, "He had been in that sad condition for so long that his will was as paralyzed as his body."[83] He had lost his will to be healed and stopped expecting change, so he embraced his lot in life.

Not only does the question of Jesus pinpoint a hindrance to true freedom, but the answer of the paralyzed man does as well. When the paralytic gets a chance to respond to the question Jesus posed about his desire for healing, the man answers by making excuses. He blames others for his inability to become healed. It is the fault of others that he has not received the healing he has wanted for thirty-eight years. He did not answer the real question. He purposefully avoided dealing with his desire for healing and moved right into the blame game. His lack of healing was not his fault, and he wanted Jesus to know this. Jesus had clearly touched a nerve with a simple question, but this man was avoiding the real issue.

This is one short theological example of how Jesus uses questions to expose the areas in people's lives that need attention. As stated before, He leverages that knowledge to equip. Jesus spent years asking questions, then equipping His disciples so He could leave and hand off the keys to the church to them.

---

83   W.W. Wiersbe, *The Bible Exposition Commentary*, Vol. 1 (Rockville: Victor Books, 1996), 304.

Before Jesus left the earth, He started releasing the disciples into ministry. In Mark 6:7, we read, "And he called the twelve and began to send them out two by two and gave them authority over the unclean spirits." In this small passage, Jesus is seen as not only releasing the disciples but also doing so by "giving them authority." Jesus began releasing the disciples into ministry by trusting them with certain tasks but also giving them the authority, or influence, to do so beforehand. Jesus, Who had the influence, began to give influence. Jesus used His own influence (i.e. authority) to gift influence on these men.

Jesus called the disciples (and, therefore, the Church as well) to go and make disciples. As Jesus ascended into Heaven, He gave His disciples the task of continuing the work He had started and to do even greater things than He himself did.[84] This is the aspect of Jesus' ministry of releasing. His work was done. It was up to the next generation to lead the church forward. He did not, however, leave the disciples with nothing to help empower them on their way. In Acts 1:8, we read, "But you will receive power when the Holy Spirit has come upon you, and you will be my witnesses in Jerusalem and in all Judea and Samaria, and to the end of the earth." Here Jesus gives the job description and the means to get it done.

In a similar way, we, too, are to seek to train those who we are leading. As stated, a good, well-trained crew can move faster, be more productive, and produce better results than a lazy, untrained crew. Questions and being a living example for our crew are vital to training them up properly. Live and lead like Jesus!

KEY TAKEAWAY PRINCIPLES

- Education is important to career growth.
- Education is important to build confidence and self-assuredness.
- Education is important to an effective outcome and a safer workplace environment.

---

[84] John 14:12

FURTHER STUDY

- "All Scripture is breathed out by God and profitable for teaching, for reproof, for correction, and for training in righteousness, that the man of God may be complete, equipped for every good work" (2 Tim. 3:16-17).
- "Train up a child in the way he should go; even when he is old he will not depart from it" (Prov. 22:6).
- "Fathers, do not provoke your children to anger, but bring them up in the discipline and instruction of the Lord" (Eph. 6:4).
- "For whatever was written in former days was written for our instruction, that through endurance and through the encouragement of the Scriptures we might have hope" (Rom. 15:4).

CHAPTER 24

DELEGATING—MAKE THE CREW PART OF THE SHIP

What is the difference between a job and career? A job is merely a series of tasks where you get paid. A career is a lifelong desire to constantly improve and build oneself at a chosen profession. Employees that are career-minded usually work hard and function more effectively.

How do you make an employee feel as though they are part of the organization and not just a hired hand? Sharing in the profits (profit-sharing) is one way to make employees stakeholders and not just salaried employees. In a nautical setting, offering the crew part of the catch or part of the treasure is a huge motivation factor. Now, they have a vested interest in the success of the mission.

There is also the important layer of delegating. If a crew member is a simple bystander watching the captain do everything, he will become lazy and reluctant to help when asked because they feel unwanted, unneeded, and useless. It is, therefore, the leader's job to maintain proper delegation.

STUDY FIRST

Read Nehemiah 3; 7:2.

LEADERS DELEGATE (NEHEMIAH 3; 7:2)

In chapter three of Nehemiah's book, we see a long list of people doing different things. This can be a boring list of names and jobs; but in it, we see a very real and practical leadership/administration principle: leaders delegate.

A leader cannot get things done alone. This is why he/she casts vision: to get others on board so they can help make the vision come to be. Without people following you, you are not a leader. A leader's job is to cast vision, then manage the vision coming to fruition.

John Maxwell says in his book, *Developing the Leaders Around You*, "A leader's success can be defined as the maximum utilization of the abilities of those under him."[85] Nehemiah could not have built a city wall by himself; to try would have been foolish. He needed people around him, and he needed to pour into these people the vision and mission of what was to come.

Nehemiah was able to rally several people to the cause and also give them specific jobs. Maxwell says that leadership is influence, and to a degree, I agree with him. I think in this type of leadership role, Nehemiah had to have a ton of God-given influence. Like Maxwell says, "Leadership is influence. Every leader has these two characteristics: (A) he is going somewhere and (B) he is able to persuade others to go with him."[86] Nehemiah needed to be able to persuade people to follow him in order for him to delegate. Again, as we can see in chapter three, he was able to do this.

Along with this idea of delegation, a leader must know who to place where. In Nehemiah 3, we see certain people doing certain jobs. Nehemiah must have known who would work best where, and so he placed them in their area of strength in order to get the job done to the best of their ability. This also means that Nehemiah knew the people he was leading well enough to put them in their areas of strength! He took the time to assess each individual to then place them where they needed to be.

This is a powerful lesson in leadership. If we are to be good leaders, we need to know the people we are leading so we can fit them into the role they can work best in!

---

85 Maxwell, *Developing the Leaders Around You*, 15.
86 Ibid, 49.

Lastly, this area of delegation shows us that each individual had their own task to complete. Not everyone can do everything, and each person needs to be assigned a specific job that only they can do. This creates unity as well as autonomy. People need to feel needed, and when they do not, they jump ship.

A perfect example of this (albeit unhealthy) was a guy named Jimmy T. on an old season of the *Survivor* show. This guy needed to be needed, and when he did not feel needed, he unwittingly sabotaged his team. He felt his gifts were not being used, so he complained and whined and brought the whole of his team to his sad level. He could not function on a team where he felt unnecessary.

Although Jimmy T. was a bit paranoid, the truth of his feelings rings true, and every leader needs to learn this lesson of people needing to feel needed. Nehemiah made sure that each person he was leading had their specific role where they could shine and do their work well.

In talking with a friend of mine, he mentioned an illustration that I think fits here. On any given "boat" (or organization), there are several types of people. There are the people rowing the boat, people sitting idly, people who are trying to row the boat backward, and people who try to drill a hole in the boat. When we delegate duties and give a common purpose, common vision, and a compelling end, we will have more boat-rowers rowing in the right direction!

KEY TAKEAWAY PRINCIPLES

- Ownership brings loyalty, trust, and motivation.
- What is the final outcome or reward?

FURTHER STUDY

- "But seek first the kingdom of God and his righteousness, and all these things will be added to you" (Matt. 6:33).
- "Now you are the body of Christ and individually members of it" (1 Cor. 12:27).

- "Then I saw a new heaven and a new earth, for the first heaven and the first earth had passed away, and the sea was no more. And I saw the holy city, new Jerusalem, coming down out of heaven from God, prepared as a bride adorned for her husband. And I heard a loud voice from the throne saying, 'Behold, the dwelling place of God is with man. He will dwell with them, and they will be his people, and God himself will be with them as their God. He will wipe away every tear from their eyes, and death shall be no more, neither shall there be mourning, nor crying, nor pain anymore, for the former things have passed away'" (Rev. 21:1-4).

CHAPTER 25

VALUE REST AND RECREATION

Remember the spiritual discipline of Sabbath? If we are properly observing Sabbath, we will find rest! Many companies have the concept of maximizing labor for the maximum profit, which usually means working the employees as hard as they can.

Most employees are familiar with the concept of burnout. Burning out the employees till they crash does not have any long-term benefits. However, if there is a short-term project where the time deadline is inflexible, it may be necessary. But in the long run, the employees will not be able to sustain that kind of workload, mentally and physically.

STUDY FIRST

Read Deuteronomy 5:12-14; Mark 2:24.

In his book *The Ruthless Elimination of Hurry*, John Mark Comer writes, "The word Sabbath comes from the Hebrew word *Shabbat*. The word literally means 'to stop.' The Sabbath is simply a day to stop: stop working, stop wanting, stop worrying, just *stop*."[87]

How often do we find ourselves *stopping*? The idea of rest and play are not always valued by individuals and are definitely not valued by companies hoping to turn a daily profit. We find ourselves in the daily grind. We quickly become overworked, overtired, and burned out.

---

87 John Mark Comer, *The Ruthless Elimination of Hurry: How to Stay Emotionally Healthy and Spiritually Alive in Our Current Chaos* (London: Hodder & Stoughton, 2019), 148.

Sabbath is built into our Christian life to help us stop working and to help us slow down and enjoy life and worshipping the Lord. Life is meant to be fun, not drab. Too often we neglect our need for rest. And in so doing, we are in disobedience to the Lord because to observe the Sabbath is a command, not a nice idea.

Some may push back and say, "Oh, that's just an Old Testament command; it's not relevant to our lives today." I am here to tell you, it is not. In Mark 2:24, Jesus declares the Sabbath was made for us. The Lord designed us, and He knows how we work best. And as the old saying goes, "Rest is best."

When we get sick, we rest. When we get worn down, we rest. Rest is recuperation. What if we rested before we needed it? What if our rest staved off sickness, burn-out, and weariness? That is exactly why Jesus said, "The Sabbath was made for man" (Mark 2:27)—because rest really does make us healthier, physically, spiritually, and emotionally.

Jesus often reflected what He recited. He not only recited the passages on the Sabbath, He also lived them. He would often get away to be alone. He would pray. He would rest, and he would worship. If Jesus Himself needed the Sabbath, why do we think we are any better?

I love Psalm 23:2 and the admonition for quiet: "He makes me lie down in green pastures. He leads me beside still waters." Being quiet is not an American norm. In fact, even going to sleep is hard for many! Getting quiet is scary; we do not want still waters or the silence of green pastures. We want busyness, noise, and hustle and bustle.

In Psalm 23, we see that David had a quiet heart that was not afraid to be made to lie down or afraid of still waters where communion with God was the only thing on the agenda. He freed himself to spend time with God, desired the deep richness of the silence, and allowed this to restore his very soul.

You see, we need the quiet in order to hear God. We need space to slow down and be in the quiet. David knew how to do this—to shut out all other voices and noises and focus laying down in the quiet to hear the voice of his Shepherd.

As leaders, we are not only to practice Sabbath for ourselves, but we are also to make room for those we lead to rest. Do not burn out your people! Find ways to get them extra time to rest. Call them to sabbath if you are in a Christian environment.

KEY TAKEAWAY PRINCIPLES

- Understand the value of rest, breaks, and vacations.
- Mind, body, and soul renewal are important.
- Avoid mental or physical burnout.
- Healthy and happy employees are more productive in the long run.

FURTHER STUDY

- "In peace I will both lie down and sleep; for you alone, O Lord, make me dwell in safety" (Psalm 4:8).
- "I lay down and slept; I woke again, for the Lord sustained me" (Psalm 3:5).
- "'Come to me, all who labor and are heavy laden, and I will give you rest. Take my yoke upon you, and learn from me, for I am gentle and lowly in heart, and you will find rest for your souls. For my yoke is easy, and my burden is light'" (Matt. 11:28-30).

CHAPTER 26
BE CAUTIOUS OF FREE TIME

The average American most likely stares at a screen when they have free time. But in the old days, sailors talked among themselves, daydreamed, or had a hobby to keep them busy. What did they talk or think about? Usually, whatever their current situation was. If things were going well, they talked about their future prosperity. If things were going badly, they talked about who was at fault and alternative decisions that should have been made.

Idleness can lead to laziness, depression, temptation, and sin. There are many popular quotes that relate to idleness, including:
- "Busy hands achieve more than idle tongues."
- "Busy mouths grow on idle heads."
- "An idle mind is a devil's workshop."
- "Boredom is the devil's delight."

I am one of those millennials who picks up their phone way too often to check their notifications. I am one of those screen-addicted people who can tend to ignore the people in front of them for the digital "community" of social media. During free time or not, I have known about this problem and have been told I have this problem, but I never *truly* admitted the problem to the inner part of my soul. I have let this acknowledgment of a problem remain on the surface, and at times, I did confess it aloud.

However, confession and repentance are two different things. We can confess to a sin and refuse to repent. We may not consciously say "I refuse to repent," but if we confess and do not repent, we will know it when we walk right back into that sin without guilt or conviction (key phrase being "without guilt or conviction"). This has been my attitude toward my tech addiction. I realize this must change.

In his book *The Ruthless Elimination of Hurry*, John Mark Comer talks about the very negative effects that tech addiction like mine can have on a person. He says that we must "let prayer set our emotional equilibrium and Scripture set our view of the world."[88] We can use our free time in much more productive ways than looking at screens!

Comer's discussion on the addiction to tech caused me to ponder these questions: what has this addiction really done to me? Why would I need to move away from such an addiction?

Let me share a few ways I engaged technology and the negative effects it has been having on my life. These are true and honest confessions. I want you to see if you can relate to some, if not all, of my journey.

I REACHED FOR MY PHONE AS SOON AS I WOKE UP.

Comer states, "The stats are ominous: 75% of people sleep next to their phones, and 90% of us check our phones immediately upon waking."[89] I was doing this constantly and still struggle from time to time. I have no room to judge you if this is you.

I allowed Facebook and all the junk that is going on or perceived to be going on in our world to start my day. I allow the world "out there" to set the tone for my emotional equilibrium. I began my day stressed. I began my day worried about the nasty comment I received on my post from the night before. I started my day thinking about how to respond to that email/message about someone's frustration with me. I chose the phone over the Bible next to my phone. I woke up focusing on anything but the Lord.

I also neglected my family right away because I just "had to" answer this message or that email. I just "had to" clarify my post. I "just had" to comment

---

[88] John Mark Comer, *The Ruthless Elimination of Hurry: How to Stay Emotionally Healthy and Spiritually Alive in Our Current Chaos* (London: Hodder & Stoughton, 2019), 229.
[89] Ibid, 228.

on someone else's post. In so doing, I was ignoring the people I had right in front of me.

Of course, none of those are things I actually *had* to do—and definitely not right away. Yet I made those things both urgent and necessary. I did that. I continue to do that. I relapsed this weekend and checked an email at home before I went to work. The email frustrated me and caused me to be a little snippy. It set the tone for my day.

AT STOP SIGNS OR STOP LIGHTS, I WOULD CHECK MY PHONE.

Anyone willing to admit this one, too? I know you are out there. I cannot be alone, can I? The same urge that caused me to look at my phone in the morning causes me to look at my phone while I am behind the wheel. My morning commute from my house to the church is four minutes at the most. Yet at almost every stop sign or stop light, I would find myself habitually checking my phone.

This is where a little science is helpful. Way back in 2016 (ha), researchers discovered this:

> Lots of studies have worked toward figuring out what exactly goes on in our brains when we're participating in social media—specifically, Facebook. A recent one discovered a strong connection between Facebook and the brain's reward center, called the nucleus accumbens. This area processes rewarding feelings about things like food, sex, money, and social acceptance. When we get positive feedback on Facebook, the feeling lights up this part of our brain. The greater the intensity of our Facebook use, the greater the reward. Another fascinating study recorded physiological reactions like pupil dilation in volunteers as they looked at their Facebook accounts to find that browsing Facebook can evoke what they call flow state, the feeling you get when you're totally and happily engrossed in a project or new skill.[90]

---

90   Courtney Seiter, "The Secret Psychology of Facebook: Why We Like, Share, Comment and Keep Coming Back," April 23, 2016, Buffer.com, https://buffer.com/resources/psychology-of-facebook.

This is why it is so hard *not* to check your phone while driving (or stopped). There is a reward system within our brain chemistry. So, we are not crazy for doing this. Yet because we do, we can notice that we have a tech addiction problem. There is no way anyone would take a risk like taking their eyes off the road while driving unless it were to fill an addictive need.

These are but two areas where my tech addiction has come into play. Challenged by John Mark Comer, I am setting some things in place.

First, I leave my phone where it is when I wake up. I do not check it. I make some coffee, let my wife sleep in, and go to the rocking chair in my living room to drink coffee and soak in the Word. Currently, I am focusing on the life of Joseph in Genesis.

Second, I do not check my email (and most of the time, Facebook) before I get into the office. These are two minor steps, and I will continue to add more, as John Mark Comer suggests twenty ways!

I share this because I do not think I am alone. I bring this up here and dig into it now because of the issue of "free time." I encourage you to read Comer's book in your free time. I think it will help you as it helped me.

KEY TAKEAWAY PRINCIPLES

- Keep the crew active and focused.
- Sports, hobbies, and activities should be encouraged (officers versus the crew).
- Idleness is not productive.

FURTHER STUDY

- "For we hear that some among you walk in idleness, not busy at work, but busybodies" (2 Thess. 3:11).
- "A slack hand causes poverty, but the hand of the diligent makes rich" (Prov. 10:4).
- "And we urge you, brothers, admonish the idle, encourage the fainthearted, help the weak, be patient with them all" (1 Thess. 5:14).

PART 5
CASE STUDIES
BY: TIM HIBSMAN

God is everywhere. Often, we distance ourselves from God. We have a work personality, a family personality, and a church personality. Our behavior, etiquette, and standards may be different in these situations; but it is important to understand that God's principles follow us everywhere.

What works, and what does not work? If something works, evaluate it and see why it works and how you can improve upon it. If something does not work, why? How do you learn from that incident? Read and evaluate the following case studies and see if the stories can be related to your life. What Christian concepts can you connect with each event? Does being a Christian give you a greater understanding of life's events—big or small?

Learning from losers sounds awkward. But if you say, "Learn from your mistakes," that sounds good. There is a famous nautical quote that says, "A ship in port is safe. But that's not what ships were built for." It is imperative to go out into the world and not be afraid to make mistakes. If possible, you want to learn from other people's mistakes before you make them. Another famous quote says, "Life is like the ocean. Waves will try to knock you down and push you back to where you started, but once you fight through them, the entire ocean is yours." The waves knocking you down are symbolic of setbacks and obstacles. It is essential to learn from, adapt to, and overcome these experiences.

CHAPTER 27
TESTING THE CAPTAIN

While on a six-day cruise with seventy passengers, the captain gave his introduction and safety speech. Part of his speech was on drug usage. Alcohol was okay. If passengers overindulged, they were instructed to puke on the leeward side (not windward). Also, the crew could easily clean up by hosing off the desk. All other drugs were prohibited.

We were sailing through both U.S. and British waters, and the U.S. Coast Guard had permission to patrol the area. There is a zero-tolerance rule in the U.S. Coast Guard, which means if they find illegal narcotics on your ship, they can seize the entire vessel. The captain made it clear that *no* drugs were allowed; and if discovered, he would confiscate the drugs, throw the violating passengers off as soon as he could, and notify the authorities.

On one particular cruise, a couple were smoking marijuana on the upper deck. The crew members were made aware and notified the captain. When he approached the couple, they responded that it was only one joint, and there was no more. As he walked away from them, I asked him if this was the end of the situation. The captain replied, "No!" Then he asked me, "Have you ever seen someone walk the plank? It's happening at five o'clock tomorrow morning."

So, I set my alarm for 4:55 a.m. The ship was at a small dock but was too big to pull alongside; so the bow was tied to the dock, and engines were in slow reverse to make sure we did not run aground. Promptly at 5:00 a.m., the crew dragged the couple from their cabin, amid yelling and screaming. The couple, wrapped in sheets, were pushed down the plank leading to the dock.

THE ANCHORED LIFE

A crew member had assembled their belongings and luggage and tossed those on the dock. The captain was at the helm, watching the entire situation. Once the couple were safely on the dock, the captain stepped forward. "I have a zero tolerance for drugs. I told you what the consequences were. I will notify the authorities. Have a nice day."

KEY TAKEAWAY PRINCIPLES

- Follow directions.
- Do not test the captain.
- If you break the rules, be prepared to take the consequences.

FURTHER STUDY

- "'You shall not put the LORD your God to the test, as you tested him at Massah'" (Deut. 6:16).
- "Jesus said to him, 'Again it is written, *You shall not put the Lord your God to the test*'" (Matt. 4:7).
- "But Ahaz said, 'I will not ask, and I will not put the LORD to the test'" (Isa. 7:12).

CHAPTER 28

SAFETY DRILLS

During the safety drills, the captain made the passengers participate in safety procedures. The most obvious one was putting on the life preservers and rallying to the evacuation areas. On our schooner, the ship would keel over under heavy sail. Often, people would try to move around with objects in their hands on this uneven deck. It was not unheard of to have a passenger fall down and slide right under the railing and go overboard. If anyone ever fell overboard, there were four steps that had to be followed. The captain made everyone repeat the steps out loud and pretend that someone had fallen overboard.

1. Keep your eyes on the person.
2. Point directly at the person.
3. Throw a life preserver.
4. Yell, "Man overboard!" as loudly as you can.

Curiously, a year later, I discovered he had changed step three. I asked why. He said a drunken man fell overboard, and over twenty passengers followed the steps precisely. It took fifteen minutes to slow the ship down, drop an anchor, and pick up the guy. It took over two hours to pick up all the life preservers.

KEY TAKEAWAY PRINCIPLES

- Keep a watchful eye.
- Learn by doing.
- People remember memorable events.

FURTHER STUDY

- "Be sober minded; be watchful. Your adversary the devil prowls around like a roaring lion, seeking someone to devour" (1 Peter 5:8).
- "I will instruct you and teach you in the way you should go; I will counsel you with my eye upon you" (Psalm 32:8).
- "All Scripture is God-breathed and is useful for teaching, rebuking, correcting and training in righteousness" (2 Tim. 3:16).

CHAPTER 29
CAPTAIN SERVING FOOD

On one beautiful afternoon in the Caribbean, we were having cheeseburgers on the beach (based on Jimmy Buffett's song, "Cheeseburger in Paradise") on an uninhabited island. The crew set up a lunch table with side dishes and condiments for the cheeseburgers. Captain Adrian was standing right next to the galley crew in the serving line. He was serving passengers and working shoulder to shoulder with his crew.

Often, the captain and officers consider themselves higher than the crew and will not degrade themselves by doing the work of crew. However, it is important for the officers to understand the duties and responsibilities of the crew. It may be necessary for the captain and officers to not only lower themselves by taking on the crew's responsibilities, but also to go even lower by serving the crew with a humble servant's heart.

KEY TAKEAWAY PRINCIPLES

- Have a servant's heart.
- Be a humble example to others.
- Respect everyone's job on board.

FURTHER STUDY

- "Humble yourselves before the Lord, and he will exalt you" (James 4:10).
- "But he gives more grace. Therefore it says, 'God opposes the proud but gives grace to the humble'" (James 4:6).

- "He leads the humble in what is right, and teaches the humble his way" (Psalm 25:9).
- "With all humility and gentleness, with patience, bearing with one another in love" (Eph. 4:2).
- "When pride comes, then comes disgrace, but with the humble is wisdom" (Prov. 11:2).
- "If I then, your Lord and Teacher, have washed your feet, you also ought to wash one another's feet. For I have given you an example, that you also should do just as I have done to you" (John 13:14-15).
- "Then he ordered the crowds to sit down on the grass, and taking the five loaves and the two fish, he looked up to heaven and said a blessing. Then he broke the loaves and gave them to the disciples, and the disciples gave them to the crowds" (Matt. 14:19).
- "Show hospitality to one another without grumbling" (1 Peter 4:9).

CHAPTER 30
NETWORKING

On one cruise, I asked the captain what he did on his days off. He replied that he liked hanging out with his friends. I pushed further about activities and friends. It ended up he liked to play tennis, squash, and cricket. His friends consisted of some local officials, including the chief of police, mayor, governor, and Coast Guard officers. Not only did he enjoy the sports and the company, but he also did an excellent job networking. It is a good idea to surround yourself with prominent people with varying skills and responsibilities.

To build up the body or the organization, Jesus provided many different people with different skills.

KEY TAKEAWAY PRINCIPLES

- You cannot do it alone.
- Find effective people for your team.
- Understand that different people have different skills.

FURTHER STUDY

- "And he gave the apostles, the prophets, the evangelists, the shepherds and teachers, to equip the saints for the work of ministry, for building up the body of Christ, until we all attain to the unity of the faith and of the knowledge of the Son of God, to mature manhood, to the measure of the stature of the fullness of Christ" (Eph. 4:11-13).

- "Two are better than one, because they have a good reward for their toil. For if they fall, one will lift up his fellow. But woe to him who is alone when he falls and has not another to lift him up! Again, if two lie together, they keep warm, but how can one keep warm alone? And though a man might prevail against one who is alone, two will withstand him—a threefold cord is not quickly broken" (Eccl. 4:9-12).
- "Iron sharpens iron, and one man sharpens another" (Prov. 27:17).

CHAPTER 31
NEEDED SOMEONE WITH A PULSE

My friend Chris was a competitive catamaran racer. He had actually built his own catamaran and would race a couple of times a year in the Southern California and San Diego areas. A local charter and sailing business was promoting the sale of smaller catamarans like Hobie Cats and asked Chris if he would compete in one of their sponsored, promotional events. Chris needed a partner and asked me to sail for one day.

I had never been on a catamaran in my life. My primary duties were to stay out of his way, and I think I was being used as a ballast. He knew exactly how to sail on one hull and how to tack sharply and effectively. I may not have been the most essential crew member, but he would have been disqualified without a partner. We competed in five short races that day and were always in the top three; however, we never got first place—not bad for my first time on a catamaran.

Spectacular, incredible, or outgoing actions are not always required. Just showing up with a willing heart may be a beginning. Consider how many people took a simple first step, such as just showing up and listening.

KEY TAKEAWAY PRINCIPLES

- Get into the race/game.
- You do not start out as an expert.
- Learn and grow as you go.
- You have a zero chance of winning if you do not show up for the race.

FURTHER STUDY

- "He who has ears to hear, let him hear" (Matt. 11:15).
- "Let the wise hear and increase in learning, and the one who understands obtain guidance" (Prov. 1:5).
- "Like a gold ring or an ornament of gold is a wise reprover to a listening ear (Prov. 25:12).
- "Incline your ear, and hear the words of the wise, and apply your heart to my knowledge" (Prov. 22:17).

CHAPTER 32
SPIT ON THE RESCUE PARTY

While talking to an old salt, the crusty, old sailor shared a factual account of a sinking ship. The pleasure schooner with about forty passengers accidentally hit a reef that cracked the hull of the ship right by the drive shaft. Water started to flood the engine room. The crew closed the hatches and sealed off the engine room so the ship would not sink. However, as the stern of the ship flooded, the bow of the ship rose in the air. Passengers had to cling to railings, masts, and anything else to keep from sliding off the deck.

Following the captain's orders, the crew sent out an SOS and then started to lighten the ship. They threw everything not nailed down overboard, including passenger luggage. Within a few hours, a French naval ship approached after receiving the distress call. The passengers were relieved.

The captain of the French naval vessel took out a bullhorn and asked if they were abandoning ship. The other captain said no because that meant the schooner would be abandoned and anyone could claim it as salvage. So, the French captain said, "Have a nice day," and started to depart.

Passengers were yelling for assistance. The French captain explained how only French citizens were allowed on a French naval vessel unless they were abandoning ship. He eventually agreed to tow the ship into a harbor to be repaired. As the passengers were finally helped from the schooner to the dock by French sailors, many of the passengers were furious that they were not allowed to board the French vessel and had to cling to the bow-up schooner. Many cursed the French vessel as they departed.

KEY TAKEAWAY PRINCIPLES

- Do not be ungrateful.
- Some people will hate you no matter what you do.
- Do not get angry.
- Understand the reasons why people do what they do.

FURTHER STUDY

- "But love your enemies, and do good, and lend, expecting nothing in return, and your reward will be great, and you will be sons of the Most High, for he is kind to the ungrateful and the evil" (Luke 6:35).
- "Whoever is slow to anger has great understanding, but he who has a hasty temper exalts folly" (Prov. 14:29).
- "Let all bitterness and wrath and anger and clamor and slander be put away from you, along with all malice" (Eph. 4:31).
- "But now you must put them all away: anger, wrath, malice, slander, and obscene talk from your mouth" (Col. 3:8).
- "A hot-tempered man stirs up strife, but he who is slow to anger quiets contention" (Prov. 15:18).

CHAPTER 33
SMOKE INHALATION

On the island of Grenada, our schooner was anchored in a quiet harbor. Most of the passengers and crew were exploring the island. I was sleeping on the beach with a view of our ship in the distance. Lunch on the ship was free—if you wanted to trek back to the dock and catch a launch. I was too relaxed in the warm sun and decided to forego lunch.

My father heard rumors of curry shrimp and headed back to the ship. While he was there with about a dozen other passengers, there was a grease fire in the galley. It was not too severe, but the smoke looked horrendous. Small fires onboard have to be dealt with quickly before they get out of hand.

The ship's fire alarm was sounded, and the crew donned their fire gear and quickly focused on the fire. However, the passengers were instructed to assemble on the top deck when the fire alarm was sounded. The galley was toward the bow of the ship, since a ship always points into the wind while at anchor. The wind blew the heavy smoke right into the assembled passengers. The crew did not even notice because they were fighting the fire.

Other crew members were ashore because the ship was not at sail. The passengers were exposed to heavy, thick smoke. Passengers were coughing and gagging, and after a few moments, they had to leave the assembly area. Smoke was everywhere, and some passengers were on the verge of panic because they were not aware of what was happening.

My father took off his life preserver, walked down the gangway to the water, and jumped in the water. Since they were in a calm harbor, he swam to the beach. When he hit the beach, he walked up to me and said, "Move over. I'm taking your towel and spot." He laid down and rested from his experience.

Seeing the smoke from the ship, I asked, "Did you abandon ship?"

He replied, "Yes."

I said, "Captain doesn't like it when passengers abandon ship without permission."

He grumbled and said, "Crew members were focusing on the ship and ignored the passengers. I don't care what any of them think."

The primary focus should be on people. Do not ignore your most important responsibilities, especially when human life may be involved. When the primary focus is money, power, or other concepts, that will lead to problems.

KEY TAKEAWAY PRINCIPLES

- Focus on people!
- Keep a watchful eye out on what your priorities are.
- Training and preparation are essential during hazardous situations.
- Actions and inaction send signals to everyone involved.

FURTHER STUDY

- "Beloved, I pray that all may go well with you and that you may be in good health, as it goes well with your soul" (3 John 2).
- "Owe no one anything, except to love each other, for the one who loves another has fulfilled the law" (Rom. 13:8).

CHAPTER 34

FOLLOWING ORDERS TO THE LETTER

One evening, I was sitting with several crew members who were from Guyana. They were drinking rum punches that were being served from the bar. I asked them about some of their experiences. One crew member said he was on a ship that had almost sunk.

The ship got too close to shore while trying to find an anchorage and hit a reef. It put a crack in the hull right beneath the engine shaft leading to the propeller. The crack rapidly flooded the engine room. The engineer secured the engine room to save the ship from sinking. However, the ship dipped below the surface at the stern of the ship, and the bow rose.

Passengers and crew were nervous but not terrified. There were plenty of life rafts. An SOS message was sent and received. Otherwise, it was a beautiful day in the Caribbean. As the passengers and crew waited for rescue, the captain ordered that everything not nailed down be thrown overboard to save the ship. The crew members literally and blindly followed the orders. The captain should have provided more specific orders, and the crew should have used some common sense.

Two problems became apparent. First, crew members threw passenger belongings overboard. At that moment, no one really cared about clothing, toiletries, and such. However, throwing their passports, money, and airline tickets overboard did not go over very well. Second, one crew member threw everything in the galley overboard. Canned goods and sealed items were not an issue. But the raw meat products that were thrown overboard started to attract some sea life. The mood on the ship quickly changed when shark fins started showing up around the ship.

Fortunately, the passengers were all rescued within a few hours. The ship was towed to shore and eventually repaired for service once again. But the mental image of shark fins circling the ship was a picture that haunted all the passengers.

KEY TAKEAWAY PRINCIPLES

- Understand the consequences of your actions.
- Know proper procedures for emergencies.
- Provide clear and concise instructions.
- In a stressful situation, it does not take much to make people panic.

FURTHER STUDY

- "Casting all your anxieties on him, because he cares for you" (1 Peter 5:7).
- "Cast your burden on the Lord, and he will sustain you; he will never permit the righteous to be moved" (Psalm 55:22).
- "Fear not, for I am with you; be not dismayed, for I am your God; I will strengthen you, I will help you, I will uphold you with my righteous right hand" (Isa. 41:10).
- "The Lord is good, a stronghold in the day of trouble; he knows those who take refuge in him" (Nahum 1:7).

CHAPTER 35
KID AT THE HELM, CREW ASLEEP

At sixteen years old, I was asked to help sail the ship. The schooner had over seventy passengers, and on that particular night, the ship was sailing between islands in the Virgin Islands. The captain wanted the ship to be in the new anchorage at sunrise so the passengers could enjoy exploring a new island right after breakfast. I was asked if I could man the helm and simply keep the ship on course while another crew member checked the sails, radar, weather, and other things.

My watch was between 11:00 p.m. and 1:00 a.m. It was a beautiful evening, and I was enjoying my quiet task at the wheel. I had not seen the other crew member since midnight. As my shift was coming to an end, I was sailing between two islands. I was not close to land, but I was nervous there might be a reef.

No one was around. In the 1980s, we did not have the best equipment, and most of it was inside the wheelhouse. I was able to reach a nautical map (which had a plastic coating on it) of the area. There was a reef on the northern island, but it was deep enough where it posed no danger. Just to be safe, I veered a southernly course.

I passed through the islands at 1:10 a.m. with no incident. It was now 1:30, and my shift had been over for thirty minutes. Still, there was no sign of my partner. Finally, just before 2:00 a.m., I was afraid something might have happened to him. I could not leave my post, since I was manning the wheel. I had to make a daring move.

I took off my shirt and used it to tie off the wheel with a mount in the deck that was used to secure the door of the wheelhouse. My plan was to run as fast as I could to the crew quarters and get some help. On my way, I passed by the galley and noticed the crew member holding a cup of coffee. He was face down on the table, sound asleep. I slapped him in the back of the head and told him, "Get to the helm. I need your help." He immediately woke up, apologizing. He woke up the next shift, and I was relieved of duty.

In the morning, after I woke up, I proceeded to get some breakfast and coffee. The captain summoned me to his table. He asked about what had happened the previous night (morning). I described the situation to him and asked if I had done anything wrong. He said I did everything perfectly.

However, on the little reef I had avoided, a ship had run aground the previous year and was under the waterline. It was possible that a bigger ship could hit it, thus endangering the ship and all her passengers and crew. I told him I was not aware of that. He said the other crew member was informed of that situation. It was a bittersweet situation. I was commended for making a good command decision. However, a sixteen-year-old boy was not supposed to make that decision. The crew member who fell asleep was fired.

KEY TAKEAWAY PRINCIPLES

- Be very cautious when giving inexperienced people great power and responsibility.
- Learn from mistakes.
- Understand the consequences of actions.

FURTHER STUDY

- "Train up a child in the way he should go; even when he is old he will not depart from it" (Prov. 22:6).
- "Fathers, do not provoke your children to anger, but bring them up in the discipline and instruction of the Lord" (Eph. 6:4).

- "Behold, children are a heritage from the LORD, the fruit of the womb a reward. Like arrows in the hand of a warrior are the children of one's youth. Blessed is the man who fills his quiver with them! He shall not be put to shame when he speaks with his enemies in the gate" (Psalm 127:3-5).
- "But Jesus said, 'Let the little children come to me and do not hinder them, for to such belongs the kingdom of heaven'" (Matt. 19:14).
- "Even a child makes himself known by his acts, by whether his conduct is pure and upright" (Prov. 20:11).
- "Children, obey your parents in everything, for this pleases the LORD" (Col. 3:20).
- "And they were bringing children to him that he might touch them, and the disciples rebuked them. But when Jesus saw it, he was indignant and said to them, 'Let the children come to me; do not hinder them, for to such belongs the kingdom of God. Truly, I say to you, whoever does not receive the kingdom of God like a child shall not enter it.' And he took them in his arms and blessed them, laying his hands on them" (Mark 10:13-16).

CHAPTER 36
DON'T HIT OUR MASTS

When I was a young teenager in the 1980s, we sailed through the Bahamas on Christmas Day. On that one day, I witnessed three drug trafficking aircraft flying overhead. This is a very popular day to smuggle drugs because law enforcement were usually not fully staffed.

It was easy to determine if the planes were carrying drugs. To enter the United States, the planes would fly very fast and under the radar. They would drop their cargo and get out of U.S. airspace before they were intercepted. These airplanes were only a few hundred feet off the water. In fact, one plane diverted its course because it was so low, the pilot was afraid he might hit our masts.

Days later, we were exploring a deserted island, and on the hillside, we saw a scorched area with an aircraft tail section sticking out. The pilot was flying at night, and he was so low, he literally ran into an island. Upon further exploration, we noticed the drugs were gone, but the remains of the plane and pilot were left behind.

KEY TAKEAWAY PRINCIPLES

- There are evil and greedy people around you.
- Understand there are consequences to one's actions.
- Sometimes, you cannot recover when you hit rock bottom (because you are dead).

FURTHER STUDY

- "Do not be overcome by evil, but overcome evil with good" (Rom. 12:21).
- "Woe to those who call evil good and good evil, who put darkness for light and light for darkness, who put bitter for sweet and sweet for bitter!" (Isa. 5:20).
- "Abstain from every form of evil" (1 Thess. 5:22).
- "A greedy man stirs up strife, but the one who trusts in the LORD will be enriched" (Prov. 28:25).

CHAPTER 37
WRAPPED IN SEAWEED

I got my scuba certification in Redondo Beach, California. Our graduation dive was off of Catalina Island. There is a very nice underwater park off the casino with several sunken ships.

Nearby was a kelp forest. Kelp is similar to the seaweed seen on the beach; but underwater, this type of seaweed, or kelp, is quite beautiful. Found close to shore off the North American shoreline, kelp is actually large, brown algae that can grow up to eighteen inches a day in relatively shallow, cold water. The kelp is attached to the seafloor, and kelp blades are very buoyant, thus extended upward toward the sunlight. The stipe (or stock) is very flexible and lets the kelp sway in the current.

I was swimming through the underwater forest examining the sea life that was living in and around the algae. The current shifted, and several of the kelp plants engulfed me. The stipes were quite strong and flexible. The more I moved, the more entangled I became. I was literally tied up by kelp.

It was a little distressing to lose my mobility and freedom of movement. If I did not have a dive knife, I would have been extremely worried, since I was low on air. Fortunately, my dive partner came over and helped to free me without killing any part of the kelp.

KEY TAKEAWAY PRINCIPLES

- Life is full of challenges. You may lose your mobility and freedom of movement.
- You never know what obstacles may be thrown at you.
- No matter what happens, trust in Jesus.

FURTHER STUDY

- "The waters closed in over me to take my life; the deep surrounded me; weeds were wrapped about my head" (Jonah 2:5).
- "'Let us burst their bonds apart and cast away their cords from us'" (Psalm 2:3).
- "When I am afraid, I put my trust in you" (Psalm 56:3).

CHAPTER 38

SLEEPING IN THE RIGGING AND SAILS

While in the Virgin Islands, our schooner would sail in the early mornings or late afternoons. All the islands were so close to each other that no long sailing voyages were necessary. In the evening, there were free rum punches, and the passengers were getting a little noisy and rowdy. On the upper deck, the mainsail was rolled up just above the boom. It was large enough for me to climb up on top and push the edges of the sail to the sides and make a little spot to lie in it. The light on the center mast gave me just enough light to read my Clive Cussler novel or spend time in God's Word. Sometimes, you just need to get away from all the noise, so seek a place to get rest for your soul and quiet your mind.

KEY TAKEAWAY PRINCIPLES

- Sometimes, you need to be alone.
- Understand the value of quiet time.
- Make sure others around you understand the importance of this solitude.

FURTHER STUDY

- "And rising very early in the morning, while it was still dark, he departed and went out to a desolate place, and there he prayed" (Mark 1:35).

- "And when it was day, he departed and went into a desolate place. And the people sought him and came to him, and would have kept him from leaving them" (Luke 4:42).
- "And after he had taken leave of them, he went up on the mountain to pray" (Mark 6:46).

CHAPTER 39
CLEAR INSTRUCTIONS

On every sailing cruise, the captain would provide clear instructions for life on board the ship. It may sound simple, but failure to comply might mean injury. For example, one of the most basic rules the captain would give passengers is to use one hand for yourself and one for the ship. On a moving ship, it is imperative that one hand is on the ship to stabilize the landlubbers. I cannot tell you how many times I have seen people lose their footing and fall on a slippery deck because they had objects in both hands. One of the captain's favorite lines was, "The ship gets priority. If you have a drink in one hand and a woman in the other, you have to sacrifice one."

KEY TAKEAWAY PRINCIPLES

- Follow the rules.
- Follow basic instructions.
- Breaking rules has consequences.
- Listen, learn, and obey.

FURTHER STUDY

- "Obey your leaders and submit to them, for they are keeping watch over your souls, as those who will have to give an account. Let them do this with joy and not with groaning, for that would be of no advantage to you" (Heb. 13:17).
- "Hear, my son, your father's instruction, and forsake not your mother's teaching" (Prov. 1:8).

- "I will instruct you and teach you in the way you should go; I will counsel you with my eye upon you" (Psalm 32:8).
- "Where there is no guidance, a people falls, but in an abundance of counselors there is safety" (Prov. 11:14).

CHAPTER 40
FLIP-FLOPS

Most people own several kinds of footwear. There are purposes for each type of shoe or boot. Hiking boots are designed very differently than evening wear shoes. It is important to know the purpose of the type of shoe you are wearing. Many people wear sandals to the beach and then kick them off when they sit down or go into the water.

The flimsiest and cheapest form of sandal are flip-flops. They are made of plastic or rubber with a thong between the big toe and second toe. Since they are not securely attached to the foot, they often cause many problems. These are especially hazardous on a ship if you are going up and down stairs, ladders, and gangways. If you are going to wear sandals, they have to strap securely around the ankle.

For safety reasons, we usually ban flip-flops from being worn on the ship. Many passengers carry them till they get to shore. If they trip and hurt themselves on shore, it is not our responsibility.

KEY TAKEAWAY PRINCIPLES

- It is hard to make progress when you are injured.
- You can move quicker and more effectively if you have the proper equipment.
- Do not overlook safety issues.

FURTHER STUDY

- "'I baptize you with water for repentance, but he who is coming after me is mightier than I, whose sandals I am not worthy to carry. He will baptize you with the Holy Spirit and fire'" (Matt. 3:11).
- "'In this manner you shall eat it: with your belt fastened, your sandals on your feet, and your staff in your hand. And you shall eat it in haste. It is the LORD's Passover" (Exod. 12:11).
- "'Even he who comes after me, the strap of whose sandal I am not worthy to untie'" (John 1:27).
- "'But the father said to his servants, *Bring quickly the best robe, and put it on him, and put a ring on his hand, and shoes on his feet*'" (Luke 15:22).
- "'That we may buy the poor for silver and the needy for a pair of sandals and sell the chaff of the wheat?'" (Amos 8:6).

CHAPTER 41
KNOW THE LEEWARD SIDE

When you are seasick, it is best to vomit over the side of the ship. Otherwise, the crew has the unfortunate job of hosing off the deck. It is not very wise to vomit into the wind because if you do, then it might be blown back into your face. Therefore, the leeward side is best—not the windward side.

Parties were very common on several of our voyages. There were several types of parties: bon voyage, stowaway, toga, captain's dinner, etc. There was also usually a good supply of liquor, especially rum from the local islands. And there was always a group of people who would overindulge and get sick. Even the next morning, there would be hungover people who would easily get sick from the motion of the ship or the smells coming from the galley. On multiple occasions, I found myself hosing off the deck. Because of this task, I am not fond of vomit or drunkenness.

KEY TAKEAWAY PRINCIPLES

- Know the importance of the leeward side (and windward side).
- Whether you like it or not, you sometimes have to associate with sick people, sinners, and drunkards.
- Learn from the poor behavior of others.

FURTHER STUDY

- "What the true proverb says has happened to them: 'The dog returns to its own vomit, and the sow, after washing herself, returns to wallow in the mire'" (2 Peter 2:22).

- "These also reel with wine and stagger with strong drink; the priest and the prophet reel with strong drink, they are swallowed by wine, they stagger with strong drink, they reel in vision, they stumble in giving judgment. For all tables are full of filthy vomit, with no space left" (Isa. 28:7-8).
- "And do not get drunk with wine, for that is debauchery, but be filled with the Spirit" (Eph. 5:18).
- "For the drunkard and the glutton will come to poverty, and slumber will clothe them with rags" (Prov. 23:21).

CHAPTER 42
PARTIES

As mentioned previously, on several of my trips, there would be shipboard parties. One was the pirates, pimps, prostitutes, and sea captains party. To attend the party, you had to dress up as one of these characters. Often, there were also toga parties, where passengers would simply take the sheets off their beds and wear them to the party.

The evening would start out with the bartender making a rum punch. Rum was extremely cheap in the area, especially if you bought it by the barrel. I was not one to participate in these activities, but they did spark my curiosity. These were not high school kids who were influenced by immaturity, stupidity, and peer pressure. These were smart, career-focused, working-class people. What was their motivation?

Some of the people drank so much, they passed out and/or had a horrible hangover. Some danced and jumped so recklessly, they sprained their ankles or bruised other parts of their bodies. Some yelled and sang so loudly that they had laryngitis and sore throats the next day. I mingled with them, trying to psychoanalyze them.

On one particular cruise, I discovered that the majority of them had high-stress jobs and careers. They would go home after partying on the cruise and deal with the stress of big mortgage payments and other personal finance issues. Of course, family issues can also cause high stress. Most of these people just wanted to release some stress. They just wanted to let go. Even if there were physical consequences the next day, they usually felt relaxed and more at ease during the party. So, my question was, is there an easier way to do this?

I pulled many all-nighters during my college days. I understood how socializing with friends after finals really helped me to unwind. The point was to understand the root causes of the situations and not just judge the first thing I saw.

Consider the biblical story of Jesus at the well with the Samaritan woman (John 4). It was pointed out that she had five husbands, and the man she was living with was not her husband (John 4:18). Keep that story in mind.

Now *assume* there is a woman whose first husband abused her, and she left. She could not find work and was literally starving, so she moved in with a different man. *Assume* she had children and could not even get a full-time job. In biblical days, there were no food banks and welfare housing. On the surface, it is easy to say she is sinful, but what are her options? Are you willing to house her, feed her, feed her kids, and help her to find employment and day care? If so—great. If not, what option are you proposing?

One of the most insensitive and possibly ignorant comments is to say, "God will provide for your needs" (Phil. 4:19) and then walk away. Will this happen instantly? What does that mean? How will that feed this woman?

What if her response is that God said do not worry about earthly desires; your treasures are laid up in Heaven (Matt. 6:19-21)? If she were to leave her benefactor, she could starve to death, but there would be glories in Heaven. Do you think she would accept that situation? Would you? Therefore, it is extremely important to *connect* with people and learn what is really going on in their lives. Just examining and commenting on the surface issues could actually make matters worse.

KEY TAKEAWAY PRINCIPLES

- Understand the motive behind people's actions and behavior.

- Do not feel pressured to participate, but be careful to not condemn or judge.
- Stress release activities are important (if done properly).

FURTHER STUDY

- "'Give your servant therefore an understanding mind to govern your people, that I may discern between good and evil, for who is able to govern this your great people?'" (1 Kings 3:9).
- "This is the day that the LORD has made; let us rejoice and be glad in it" (Psalm 118:24).
- "A time to weep, and a time to laugh; a time to mourn, and a time to dance" (Eccl. 3:4).
- "Praise the Lord! Praise God in his sanctuary; praise him in his mighty heavens! Praise him for his mighty deeds; praise him according to his excellent greatness! Praise him with trumpet sound; praise him with lute and harp! Praise him with tambourine and dance; praise him with strings and pipe! Praise him with sounding cymbals; praise him with loud clashing cymbals! Let everything that has breath praise the Lord! Praise the Lord!" (Psalm 150:1-6).
- "'Judge not, and you will not be judged; condemn not, and you will not be condemned; forgive, and you will be forgiven'" (Luke 6:37).

CHAPTER 43
RELATABLE STORIES

Soon after boarding a ship, the captain should cover safety procedures. One of my favorite captains, Captain Adrian, had a unique safety speech. He used humor to introduce a topic and then became very serious when it came to action and implementation. This back-and-forth method was great in making passengers remember the topic.

One passenger asked about the pointy spines on a sea urchin. The captain responded, "It is widely believed that urine will deaden the pain of a sea urchin's spine. So, if you step on one, feel free to buy your friend a drink or two or three and get them to help you out. However, as soon as you can, make sure you get proper medical treatment from one of the crew members."

One passenger asked about the dangers of sea creatures, like sharks. The captain responded, "Most sea beasties, like sharks and barracudas, only eat critters one-fourth or smaller than themselves. So if you see a twenty-foot barracuda, time to panic!"

KEY TAKEAWAY PRINCIPLES
- Understand the power of parables and storytelling.
- Know your audience.
- Good teachers know how to make important concepts stick in their pupils' minds.

FURTHER STUDY

- "This was to fulfill what was spoken by the prophet: 'I will open my mouth in parables; I will utter what has been hidden since the foundation of the world'" (Matt. 13:35).
- "Then the disciples came and said to him, 'Why do you speak to them in parables?' And he answered them, 'To you it has been given to know the secrets of the kingdom of heaven, but to them it has not been given'" (Matt. 13:10-11).
- "As they heard these things, he proceeded to tell a parable, because he was near to Jerusalem, and because they supposed that the kingdom of God was to appear immediately" (Luke 19:11).

CHAPTER 44

LEADERSHIP FAILURE: CASE STUDY OF KING SAUL

BY: MARV NELSON

We have all read or at least heard about King Saul in our lifetime somewhere along the way. He was a king who was good in most respects, until he started messing up. Then, his leadership took a nosedive. Although Saul's story deviates from the nautical theme, it is an important port at which to stop. This small port stop gives us a good, clean window into what *not* to do as a leader. Whether a captain of a ship, the pastor of a church, or the king of the nation of Israel, a leader needs to be careful of the pitfalls that can come with being in charge.

Only five chapters after we read that Saul was anointed as king, we read that God said of him, "'I regret that I have made Saul king, for he has turned back from following me and has not performed my commandments'" (1 Sam. 15:11).

That is not a social media fan page worthy of following. God regrets His decision to make Saul king. That is some hurtful stuff. Saul must have really stunk.

In his illustrious tour as king, Saul shows so many leadership failures that one simply must dig into them in order to learn what *not* to do as a leader. This generation needs authentic leadership. It can learn from Saul's failures. Here is the beginning of the end of Saul:

> And Samuel came to Saul, and Saul said to him, "Blessed be you to the LORD. I have performed the commandment of the LORD." And Samuel said, "What then is this bleating of

the sheep in my ears and the lowing of the oxen that I hear?" Saul said, "They have brought them from the Amalekites, for the people spared the best of the sheep and of the oxen to sacrifice to the LORD your God, and the rest we have devoted to destruction" (1 Samuel 15:13-15).

FAILURE NUMBER ONE: OWNERSHIP FAILURE

One of the things that Saul continued to do throughout his life is put the blame on other people. He rarely owned up to his issues or his mistakes. The real kicker in this story that always cracks me up is his façade with Samuel. He pretends to be super happy to see Samuel and brags about himself and the marvelous job he did by doing what God asked him to do.

Saul is so worried about his image (which we will get to in the next leadership failure) that he runs up to Samuel to prove his worth. He knows he did not do as he was asked, yet he does this in order to save face and to attempt to fool Samuel.

When Samuel calls him out on the spot about how he neglected to listen to the Lord, Saul immediately shifts blame and states, "'They have brought them from the Amalekites, for the people spared the best of the sheep and of the oxen to sacrifice to the LORD your God, and the rest we have devoted to destruction'" (1 Sam. 15:15).

He blames the people. He was willing to take credit with Samuel when he thought he could make Samuel think that the sacrifice was good but does not own up to the failure! The Scripture clearly states it was Saul *and* the people (1 Sam. 15:8-9), not just the people! Sadly, this is not an abnormal occurrence among leaders. It often occurs in every sphere of leadership, and it is something from which we need to learn.

We leaders need to be the first ones to own up to a problem. We should be in the front, honestly waving our hands when someone asks who is responsible. In my experience, I fear that way too often, pastors (and all

Christians, for that matter) are like Saul in that we cover up our mess, and when it gets pointed out, we attempt to pass the buck.

When things go bad, it is easy to point the finger and say, "The board wouldn't allow me to make changes" or "The church members are too old to move, so we stayed stagnant" or "I have too many office hours to fill, so I don't spend time in the community."

Leaders *must* own up to problems. When the people we lead see us owning up to our failures, they can feel free to own up to theirs. When we admit our junk as it is—junk—we can get free of it and grow. However, if we neglect to own responsibility, nothing will change because we will continue to sweep it under the carpet and pretend it does not exist.

Good leaders own up to failures and seek to make it right. This sad story of Saul's leadership failure was the beginning of the end for our man Saul because at the end of this story, we find that God regretted making Saul king. "Then Samuel went to Ramah, and Saul went up to his house in Gibeah of Saul. And Samuel did not see Saul again until the day of his death, but Samuel grieved over Saul. And the LORD regretted that he had made Saul king over Israel" (1 Sam. 15:34-35).

I know for sure that I struggle with this leadership failure. I fail to own up to my mess-ups. I try to pin the tail on some other donkey, but no donkey fits my tail quite like I do. I have been trying to work on it, and I have been trying to be more authentic with everyone around me and those who are following me.

I want to be the type of leader God loves and desires to be in leadership. I do not desire to be the self-absorbed leader that so many people turn into (and I myself have been!). It is tough owning up to our failures; and as leaders, it is tough when we have to swallow our followers' mistakes and own those, too. But it must be done!

Leadership is a big task, and my generation, as we come into leadership, has the potential to change the face of leadership forever. Open and authentic leadership gives more room to work on the real issues, rather than beating around the bush about non-essential things. Too many corporations and churches have had meeting after meeting trying to work on issues that do not even matter because the leaders were not transparent enough to openly admit when and where they are wrong.

If a leader fails, they need to own up to it, apologize, learn from it, and deal with that issue before they try to tackle some other issue. Also, shifting blame in this process only serves to derail the leader's ability to lead. If a leader blames someone from this generation for something they did not do, whether or not they know it was actually the leader's fault, you have lost the faith and trust of that person. That may not seem like such a big deal now, but for the sake of the company's future, if that is done time and time again, there will be little-to-nothing in way of leadership within that company or church! Take this one from Saul's book of tricks and *burn* it! May we all learn from his failures and choose within our hearts not to do the same!

FAILURE NUMBER TWO: LISTENING FAILURE

If I am honest, this is probably one of the biggest struggles I have in leadership. It is one of those leadership failures that attacks me, and you rarely know it has taken a hold of you. It is a leadership failure that only close friends can point out, and only they can walk beside you and help you conquer it. It is all about to whom we listen and whom we desire to please.

Too often in my life, as I admitted earlier, I want everyone to be happy. I want all the people who surround me in leadership, those above and below me, to be happy with my performance. I hate criticism, and I dread upsetting people. This is something on which I am working. It is something God is refining in me, so when I share Saul's failure here, I am very aware that I am looking in the mirror and telling my own story, as well as telling myself the answer to getting over this failure. Here is where Saul starts his downward spiral in his position as king over Israel.

> He waited seven days, the time appointed by Samuel. But Samuel did not come to Gilgal, and the people were scattering from him. So Saul said, "Bring the burnt offering here to me, and the peace offerings." And he offered the burnt offering. As soon as he had finished offering the burnt offering, behold, Samuel came. And Saul went out to meet him and greet him. Samuel said, "What have you done?" And Saul said, "When I saw that the people were scattering from me, and that you did not come within the days appointed, and that the Philistines had mustered at Michmash, I said, 'Now the Philistines will come down against me at Gilgal, and I have not sought the favor of the LORD.' So I forced myself, and offered the burnt offering" (1 Sam. 13:8-12).

Saul was supposed to wait for Samuel. Saul had instructions to wait, but Saul did not wait. After he does what he should not have done, Samuel calls him out. "What have you done?" (1 Sam. 13:11). Saul then shows to whom he would rather listen.

Saul saw his followers, his army, and his trusted men going back home. He realized that they were not pleased with him and what he was doing at the moment. The people did not want to sit around and wait for Samuel so they could worship God. The people wanted to get away from that place, and they were not happy that Saul waited.

Some probably tested his kingship. "Look at this *king* waiting around like a puppy dog for a *prophet*! Who rules whom? Who is really in charge here—Samuel or Saul?"

The attitude and the voices of the people rang louder in Saul's ears than did the voice of God. So, Saul scrambled to make the people happy. He sped up the process and made a sacrifice to God on his own, even though he was supposed to wait.

Saul was worried about the people's feelings toward him, and Saul was also worried about Samuel. When Samuel came, Saul revealed his heart for trying to make the people happy, and he also tried to blame it on God as an afterthought. He said, *"'The Philistines had mustered at Michmash . . . Now the*

Philistines will come down against me at Gilgal, and I have not sought the favor of the LORD. So I forced myself, and offered the burnt offering'" (1 Sam. 13:11b-12).

In an effort to appease Samuel, Saul said he was worried that if he did not please God with this sacrifice, the Philistines would be allowed to crush God's people. He also said, "I made myself do it. Samuel, I struggled, and I really did not want to. You have to see that! I forced myself to disobey God because I thought I would die if I did not!"

Saul needed to worry more about God's command than he did the grumbling and leaving of the people. We as leaders need to do the same. Our heart's desire should be to please our Father, not His people. As shepherds entrusted to steward His flock, we should not listen to the bleating of the sheep but to the whisper of our Lord.

Again, as I shared above, I struggle with this failure more than any other. I get frustrated at myself when I notice myself doing it. I pander; I appease; I lie; and I wriggle out of things—all in an effort to make people happy. If I do not know an answer to something, I have even made up stuff in an effort to have people think highly of me.

But I cannot worry about other people's opinions. I cannot worry about what *they* think. I need to be close to the Father so I can hear what He desires me to do and then do it! I do what He asks of me, even if people get upset, do not understand, jeer at me, or even leave my side because the only voice that matters and that I need to listen to is His voice!

It can be so easy to please the crowd. It can be so easy to "go with the flow," but it can be very difficult to go upstream, against the current. Sometimes (more often than not), God calls us to go upstream and go after things that may make other people upset. He often calls us to step on people's toes (in His name, of course) to wake them up from their slumber. Sheep like to slumber, and as the shepherds, we need to wake them up! The following is some practical advice in order to avoid this leadership failure:

LEADERSHIP FAILURE: CASE STUDY OF KING SAUL 229

1. Yield our desires to the Holy Spirit.
2. Be ever ready to listen to His voice.
3. Be diligent to be in the Word to hear from our Chief Shepherd
4. When God directs, we follow, no matter who may get upset.

Maybe you are wondering why there is so much "spiritual jargon" in a book on leadership. Well, I have learned as a leader that I need a Leader above any others. I find that the best leaders are those who are good at being led themselves.

As I have grown up, I have seen leaders who would not be led and only desired to create their own kingdoms, both in and out of the Church. I, like many in my generation, am tired of seeing leaders care more about their own fame and fortune than the people they are leading. As millennial leaders, in order to leverage our different style, we need to throw away the old, tattered forms of leadership and create a new form.

Saul collaborated with no one on how to lead, and it ended up making his leadership one big failure. We must create new ways to lead. A leader dependent on God, who cares more about His voice than the voice of the people, is exactly what the future of the Church and the world needs. We do not need any more pandering leaders who seek to please the people and end up in a swarm of lies. We need leaders who are authentic and real, who admit their weaknesses, and who harness the strengths of those around them, not fearing replacement but loving the progress of the whole organization.

FAILURE NUMBER THREE: APPRENTICE FAILURE

We are not done with Saul yet because the more I read his story, the more blunders I find. It is absolutely amazing to me how many failures he actually had in his leadership. Several of the failures are similar and end up coming down to the same problem.

This next leadership failure is no different. Once Saul went down this path, he continued to make this failure his lifestyle. In fact, this failure, from this point forward, defined the rest of his career.

One of the best new leadership models is the model of apprenticeship. It is a model which encourages leaders to reproduce themselves in younger, emerging leaders. It challenges the old guys to seek out young guys who will bring new life, new vision, and new direction to the companies and churches they are leading. It is an exciting movement in the leadership world, which will help make the future of those companies and churches brighter and more vibrant. It is also where Saul failed the most in his leadership.

Saul loved the spotlight. He loved the accolades that were poured onto him as king. Saul loved power, prestige, and flattery. Anything or anyone who made him feel inferior was something to be pounced on like a lion. He did not want to be outshone, nor did he desire to share the glory with any man, or even God. He took credit, owned the glory for himself, and tried to kill those who may have interfered with his glory.

This was the case with David. At first, Saul was relieved when David appeared on the scene. David killed Goliath, but when David started gaining more fans, Saul got a bit peeved.

> And the women sang to one another as they celebrated, "Saul has struck down his thousands, and David his ten thousands." And Saul was very angry, and this saying displeased him. He said, "They have ascribed to David ten thousands, and to me they have ascribed thousands, and what more can he have but the kingdom?" And Saul eyed David from that day on ... And Saul hurled the spear, for he thought, "I will pin David to the wall." But David evaded him twice. Saul was afraid of David because the LORD was with David but had departed from him ... And when Saul saw that David had great success, he stood in fearful awe of him" (1 Sam. 18:7-9, 11-12, 15).

Saul had messed up as king, so God left Saul and stopped giving him favor. Due to Saul's wicked and unrepentant heart, God was forced to choose another king. God chose David and began showering favor upon David, and His Spirit rested upon him.

This success clearly upset Saul. Instead of celebrating that God was giving Israel a better king, Saul became jealous and sought to end David's life, further separating himself from the Lord and the Lord's will.

I will be the first to admit that as a leader, it is hard to see those under you achieving success. It is hard, not because I am so great but because my sinful nature wants to be better than they. We judge ourselves in comparison to others. I have even found myself wondering why someone on social media has more "friends" than I do. That is pretty low and pathetic!

However, we all are jealous of other's success, are we not? Someone gets promoted over us—we get annoyed. Someone younger gets more accolades for their effort than we do—we get upset because, after all, we have been doing it longer!

I am learning that true, honest leadership develops others' potential. A strong leader may be effective for thirty or forty years, but if they invest in the up-and-comers, they celebrate the success of a younger person and seek to make that person better. They are investing for much longer. When we apprentice, our skills and gifts sometimes get transferred, so even when we die, we are still a part of that younger leader's life. Our influence goes further.

Saul sought only his glory, and so he jealously kept all his leadership abilities to himself. There was no attempt to teach a younger guy how to be king. He hated the success of David, and the moment it looked like David was blessed by God to take the throne was the moment Saul went ballistic.

We leaders need to be seeking how to invest in the future, even if someone eclipses us in the process, especially in the Church! It is not about us; it is about Him! As the king over Israel, Saul was supposed to be pointing the whole nation to God. Instead, he was trying to point them to himself. His reign was all about his glory, not God's glory. Saul cared more about his image than he did the image of God. Brothers and sisters, we cannot be like Saul!

I fail here a ton. I have been a people-pleaser too often, and I want people to like me. I want the glory. I want the spotlight. However, I must die to myself and start pointing upward toward God. My gifts are His gifts; my ministry is His ministry; and my wisdom is His wisdom. My friends, we are simply stewards of all He has given us.

Saul failed in developing an apprentice. We should not fail here. God has entrusted our leadership roles to us to not only lead now, but also to lead when we are gone. We must look and see who the young leaders are who have the Lord's anointing on them. How can we pick them out and apprentice them for what God has for them in the future?

I know for my situation that during the most critical years of needing to be "apprenticed," I was left to flounder on my own, to find my own way in some respects. Thankfully, God had placed around me a network of mentors outside of my workplace who poured heavily into me and made me the man and leader I am today.

The temptation to think you will live forever is simply too strong for many boomers, and they have not, in many ways, invested much into apprenticeship of the younger generations. As millennials in leadership, we need to ensure we change that for the generations under us. We have learned through watching current leaders, church or otherwise, that the most important thing is maintaining your power and influence as a leader, and that means you keep all the controls. Apprenticeship teaches others how to be effective leaders, and in some respects, it means replacing yourself.

Jesus apprenticed the twelve disciples. He taught them reliance on the Spirit, dependence upon God's provision, and His teaching style. They were invited into His every-day life. He mentored them and shaped them into the masterful men of God they became. Why would we leaders do anything different?

PART 6
SURVIVING OCEAN HAZARDS AND SHIPWRECKS

BY: TIM HIBSMAN

One of the most popular questions for non-Christians to ask is, "Why would a loving God allow this to happen?" To be honest with you, God's plan is not always clear and immediately understandable. Challenges and hardships often help us to grow in our spiritual journey. It is also possible that some of these hardships and experiences are for the benefit of others, so the focus should not always be on ourselves. However, there are some examples of positive outcomes.

After reading the following sections, the Questions to Consider section will help to put you in these situations. I have given a brief summary of each source and want you to dig deeper. How would you behave? Would you use the biblical principles in your decisions? Put your Christian thinking caps on and consider these questions. Feel free to use the Scripture references used in earlier sections.

CHAPTER 45
ROBINSON CRUSOE

In 1719, Daniel Defoe published his story of a young and impulsive Englishman who defies his parents' wishes and takes to the seas, seeking adventure. The young man is shipwrecked and cast away on a remote tropical island for twenty-eight years. Robinson saves a savage from death. The savage is named Friday and becomes his servant. Robinson teaches him the English language, civilized behavior, and Christian values.

This is a classic tale of adventure featuring cannibals, captives, and mutineers. This story may be based on real events of a Scottish castaway who survived four years on a Pacific island or a political surgeon castaway from a Caribbean penal colony.

QUESTIONS TO CONSIDER

Robinson Crusoe was looking for adventure, and he found it. Life rarely follows a structured plan. Consider these discussion questions:

- Has your career, family, or academic course (or plan) veered off into another direction?
- Do you think God was responsible for that change?
- In a tough situation, would you do better alone or with a group of people?
- Fear can be overwhelming, especially when it deals with cannibals and mutineers. How do you deal with fear?
- What would you pray for?
- If your prayer is not answered, what would you pray for next?

CHAPTER 46
LIFEBOAT

Alfred Hitchcock's 1944 movie entitled *Lifeboat* is based on John Steinbeck's novella. Several passengers survive after their ship is attacked by a German U-boat in the mid-Atlantic. Among the passengers are a purser, a stoker, a millionaire, an aristocrat, and a woman who survived with her baby. None of them are very good at manning or navigating the lifeboat.

Before their ship sank, it managed to sink the U-boat. They rescue a German sailor who cannot speak English, and other passengers do not trust him. Eventually, they discover that he speaks perfect English and is actually the U-boat's captain. Some passengers succumb as they try to sail the lifeboat to the West Indies. All the passengers are faced with difficult decisions that will reveal their true nature.

QUESTIONS TO CONSIDER

These passengers ended up learning new things about themselves. Imagine that you were one of the passengers stuck on this lifeboat. Consider these questions:

- What would you do?
- How would you act?
- Have you ever been in a life-and-death situation?
- Would you panic?
- What keeps you calm?
- Most people go into survival mode. What does that mean to you?
- Of course, the situation is chaotic. At what point would you pray?

- How would you pray?
- The Bible says, "Love your enemies" (Matt. 5:44). Could you love the Nazi sailor who is working against you?

CHAPTER 47
ABANDON SHIP

In this 1957 film, the luxury liner the *Crescent Star* sinks, and one of the ship's officers (Tyrone Power) finds himself in charge of one of the lifeboats. The boat is only built for nine people, but there are twenty desperate and injured passengers clinging for help. With a massive storm approaching, the lifeboat cannot survive the storm with so many passengers weighing it down. The officer must make the agonizing decision on who remains and who is cast off from the boat—leading to certain death.

QUESTIONS TO CONSIDER

This movie offers some great thought-provoking ideas. Put yourself in the officer's position and answer these questions:

- To save many, would you sacrifice a few?
- Could you make these kinds of life-and-death decisions?
- Would you sacrifice yourself?
- Would you sacrifice yourself if it meant your loved ones could stay onboard?
- Would you sacrifice yourself for strangers?
- Instead of drowning, what if people were not going to Heaven? Would you try to save them? How hard would you try?

CHAPTER 48
"THE OPEN BOAT"

"The Open Boat" is a short story written by Stephen Crane in 1897 based on his own experiences being shipwrecked. During the night, the ship sinks, and only four survivors are drifting in a rickety dinghy off the coast of Florida.

For two days, the exhausted and injured men struggle to keep the small boat afloat. They are constantly bailing out water and struggling with ocean swells. The little boat is so unstable that when a seagull lands on its side, they are afraid to shoo it away because it might rock the boat enough to let water come in.

Finally, they spot land. As they get nearer, they see a lighthouse. However, no one spots them. The surf is so high and rough, they are not sure they have the energy to swim to shore once their boat is capsized by the waves.

For another day, they drift, hoping to be spotted and rescued—but to no avail. They finally decide that they have to risk it. As expected, the ship capsizes, and the men struggle to make it to shore. Some are lucky enough to make the beach, while others are not so lucky.

QUESTIONS TO CONSIDER

The most intriguing part of the story is that these shipwrecked men make it within sight of the beach, but that is not close enough.

- Have you ever been within sight of your goal but not quite there? Usually, the anticipation increases, and hopefully, an adrenaline rush occurs.
- Have you ever been within sight of your goal and did not make it?

- Life does not always go in the direction you want it to go. How do you react when life throws you a curve?
- How difficult is it to remember and realize that God has a plan for you?

CHAPTER 49
PAUL'S SHIPWRECK (ACTS 27-28)

This is a wonderful illustration of God offering salvation to all who will receive it. Deliverance was provided to Paul and his shipmates. Most of the people on the ship trusted in the captain and themselves to get them to their destination. Eventually, they had no hope in themselves, the captain, or the crew. There was nothing they could do to save themselves.

Initially, they may have had confidence in their prosperity, good health, and intelligence. But they ignored the signs and warnings (from Paul), and life overwhelmed them. Jesus is the only Person Who could save them. People who trust in Him will be delivered from the storms.

QUESTIONS TO CONSIDER

Throughout his life, Paul suffered many things for the sake of the Gospel. If we are following Christ, we, too, will suffer. But Paul offers us hope in the trials.

- Have you ever been in a life-and-death situation?
- Have you ever seen someone panic?
- Have you ever prayed in difficult situations?
- What did you pray for?
- Once the situation is over, did you praise and thank God?
- How long after the situation did you acknowledge and thank God?
- Paul was obviously stressed and weak, but he stayed the course. Do you think you could have done this?

- Have you ever had lack of sleep and food for over two weeks? How did you perform? What was your attitude?
- Would you have swam for the beach? Or would you have helped others first?
- The surf was extremely powerful (it destroyed the stern of the ship). Have you ever been forced underwater or knocked over by a wave? What does a near-drowning feel like?
- Paul was in at least three shipwrecks (2 Cor. 11:25). Why do you think God caused him to have this experience so many times?

PART 7
CHRISTIAN CONCEPTS IN BOOKS AND MOVIES

Christians must live in the world. Notice how some of the great nautical books and movies implement many of the nautical principles we have examined in earlier chapters. As you go through this section, ask yourself how you would act in these situations. Did the characters act in a godly or biblical way? If not, what were the consequences? Often, many of the characters had to make hard choices (just like Christians). The biblical principles can help to make the right choices.

CHAPTER 50
THE OLD MAN AND THE SEA

Ernest Hemingway wrote *The Old Man and the Sea* in 1952. It tells the story of a battle between an old, experienced fisherman named Santiago and a large marlin. Santiago has gone eighty-four days without catching a fish and is now seen as unlucky in his village. His young apprentice Manolin is forbidden by his parents to sail with him and has been told to fish with more successful fishermen. The young boy visits Santiago every night talking about baseball, fishing, luck, and other subjects.

On the eighty-fifth day, Santiago's unlucky streak ends. He hooks a great marlin. Unable to pull it into the boat, the marlin pulls him for two days and nights. Santiago is injured but expresses a compassionate and respectful appreciation for his adversary. On the third day, Santiago uses his remaining strength to pull the fish to the side of the boat and stab it with a harpoon. Exhausted and almost delirious, Santiago thinks about the high price the fish will bring him at market and how many people will be fed.

On the way back to shore, sharks are attracted to the blood in the water and start eating the marlin. Santiago kills a shark with his harpoon but eventually loses it. He makes a new one out of his knife, but there are just too many sharks. Upon reaching the shore before dawn, he carries his heavy mast on his shoulder, leaving the skeletal remains of the fish next to his boat. Once home, he knows that he is defeated, slumps onto his bed, and falls fast asleep.

The Old Man and the Sea is famous for the Christian comparisons and allusions in the story. Here are some examples of concepts Hemingway created:

- Santiago serves as the god figure. He is powerful (he kills sharks and a marlin). He is a caretaker and apprentice to Manolin.
- The mast is a representation of the cross.
- Every night, Santiago carried the mast on his shoulder up to his house. The mast fell several times, representing Christ's struggle carrying the cross.
- Santiago bloodies his hands from the rope, showing a comparison with Christ's stigmata (the wounds in His palms).
- Manolin represents the generation that witnessed the story and shares it with future generations.
- Santiago refers to the fish as his brother, symbolizing Cain killing his brother.
- Santiago's primitive weapon (the harpoon made out of a knife) against overwhelming odds (ocean full of sharks) can be seen as symbolic of David and Goliath.
- Santiago crosses the established fishing limits and regrets it later, just as Adam and Eve crossed the boundaries and entered into sin.
- The name Santiago is derived from the Spanish form of Saint James. James had a similar martyred ending.

QUESTIONS TO CONSIDER

- Are biblical principles constantly in your life?
- Where can you see God in your life?
- Does the story become more important and interesting when you understand the subtext?
- Santiago is considered a tragic hero. Is Christ considered a tragic hero?

CHAPTER 51
SUBMARINE MOVIES AND BOOKS

There are many great movies and books that give us an idea of what life is like on a submarine. Some that I recommend are *Das Boot, U-571, Operation Petticoat, Phantom, Up Periscope, The Hunt for Red October,* and *Run Silent, Run Deep.*

Every inch of the submarine is utilized. Space is precious onboard. Sometimes, there are not enough beds for everyone, so the submariners share bunks. This is called "hot racking." Night and day are indistinguishable. Most crews alternate eight-hour shifts. The mess often rotates breakfast, lunch, and dinner so the different shifts can have variety in their meals. Sleep is at a premium, so crew members learn how to be quiet as to not wake up other crew members who are on differing shifts. All crew members are cut off from the outside world, meaning no communication, no sunlight, and no fresh air.

After the Covid-19 self-quarantine, many people felt confined and restricted to their homes. Many people have a feeling of confinement in their offices, cubicles, and study spaces. New inmates go through a confinement adjustment when they are placed in their cells for the first time. Often confinement is referred to as incarceration. Imagine being confined (or imprison or incarcerated) inside a submarine's hull that is under extreme pressure?

QUESTIONS TO CONSIDER

- Paul and Silas were in prison (Acts 16:16-40). They were incarcerated and imprisoned away from their loved ones (just like submariners). What did they do while they were in prison? How did they continue to worship God?

- Paul was under house arrest (Acts 28:17-31). How did he occupy his time? How did he continue to worship God?
- Paul was probably under house arrest for up to two years (Acts 28:30-31). Could you imagine being locked in a house for that long? What would you do? How would you praise and worship God?

CHAPTER 52

MASTER AND COMMANDER: THE FAR SIDE OF THE WORLD[91]

In 1805, Jack Aubrey takes command of the *HMS Surprise* as her captain. He begins an unlikely friendship with Stephen Maturin, the ship's surgeon. Both men have very different personalities, beliefs, and approaches to life. Their friendship builds and endures while they are ordered to hunt down and capture a powerful French vessel off the coast of South America.

QUESTIONS TO CONSIDER

These two men are forced together on a journey to the other side of the world. God often thrusts interesting people into our lives.

Consider the unique personal relationships between each of these people mentioned in the Bible:

- Saul (Paul) and Barnabas (Acts 13)
- Paul and Timothy (Phil. 2:19-23)
- Barnabas and John Mark (Acts 13:13; Col. 4:10)
- Paul and John Mark (Acts 15:36-41)
- Joseph and Pharaoh (Gen. 41)

---

91 *Master and Commander: The Far Side of the World*, directed by Peter Weir (Beverly Hills, CA: Twentieth Century Fox, 2003), DVD.

CHAPTER 53
MOBY DICK

Captain Ahab has an obsession and vendetta against the great white whale, Moby Dick, that was responsible for taking his leg. Ahab sets out on a treacherous voyage aboard *Pequod*. With reckless abandon, Captain Ahab leads his crew on his obsessive quest to a final meeting with the legendary white whale.

QUESTIONS TO CONSIDER

- The giant white whale has many similarities to Jonah's whale (Jonah 1-4).
- This had to be a traumatic situation.
- Do you think Jonah thought about the whale later in his life?
- Do you think he had dreams about the whale?
- Do you think he thought about other possible endings to this ordeal?
- What if it was longer than three days (Jonah 1:17)? Would that have had any more influence on Jonah? How many days before Jonah was pushed over his limit?
- Jonah was in a great storm prior to meeting the whale (Jonah 1:4). What do you think Jonah was thinking? Could he be thinking, how could this get any worse?
- There has been speculation that the whale's stomach acid might have altered Jonah's skin color. Do you think that was in God's plan? How could that be beneficial?

- Another key point was Captain Ahab's obsession. Consider the word *obsession* and these biblical examples:
  - 1 John 2:15-17
  - Matthew 6:24
  - Mark 7:20-23
  - Philippians 4:8

CHAPTER 54
DOWN PERISCOPE

Lieutenant Commander Tom Dodge is offered the captain's seat on a decrepit, World War II diesel submarine with the intent to simulate enemy attacks in war game exercises. His nemesis helps to handpick a motley crew of misfits to make his command more complicated.

QUESTIONS TO CONSIDER

- The captain and crew receive an undesirable mission. They are all reluctant to participate in the exercise, but they must follow orders. God often provides orders that are not favorable with people.
- How did Jonah follow God's original order to go to Nineveh (Jonah 1:1-3)?
- What other people in the Bible had problems with God's instructions?
- God may send you on a mission, and you are not welcomed. In fact, you may be persecuted (Matt. 10:14). How are you to act and feel? God's purpose for this may not be clear. Could you still shake it off without it affecting you?
- Matthew was a tax collector (Matt. 9:9). Mary Magdalene was demon-possessed at one time. Jesus used all kinds of people. Sometimes, you might have to work with a motley crew for the goodness of God. What experiences do you have working with fellow Christians for the glory of God?

CHAPTER 55
THE CAINE MUTINY

The Caine Mutiny was the 1951 Pulitzer Prize-winning novel by Herman Wouk that was turned into a movie in 1954. The old, dilapidated, World War II ship *USS Caine* gets some new crew members. Lieutenant Commander Queeg takes command, along with a young ensign named Willie Keith.

During the voyage, Lieutenant Thomas Keefer intensifies rumors and suspicions about the captain's erratic and irrational behavior. The crew starts to think he is unsuited for the position of captain. During a horrific storm, the executive officer feels he has to relieve Captain Queeg of his duties to save the ship. He and Ensign Keith are tried for mutiny in a U.S. Navy court.

QUESTIONS TO CONSIDER

The best way to prove their innocence was to let the ship sink. However, that was not a viable option. How can you deal with bad leaders? Consider these biblical situations involving poor leadership decisions:

- Pontius Pilate at the trial of Jesus (Matt. 27:24)
- Herod Antipas at the birth of Jesus (Matt. 2)
- Darius with Daniel in the den of lions (Dan. 6)
- King Nebuchadnezzar with Shadrach, Meshach, and Abednego in the furnace (Dan. 3)
- King David with Bathsheba (2 Sam. 11)

CONCLUSION
CLOSING THE SHIP'S LOG

Connections is the key word. Through many anecdotal stories and concepts, hopefully, you could see the connection between the nautical world and Christian theology. Franklin Delano Roosevelt once said, "A smooth sea never made a skilled sailor."[92] The wisdom in this statement contains truth for the Christian who must learn and grow in an often-hostile world.

We must not be afraid to take our Christian faith and take on the world. We can end our journey by dropping anchor and securing our vessel. "We have this as a sure and steadfast anchor of the soul, a hope that enters into the inner place behind the curtain" (Heb. 6:19).

---

92 "Franklink D. Roosevelt›Quotes›Quotable Quote," Goodreads.com, Accessed September 30, 2022, https://www.goodreads.com/quotes/1324527-a-smooth-sea-never-made-a-skilled-sailor.

BIBLE STUDY TIPS AND SUGGESTIONS

For Bible study or Sunday school classes, there are several different ways to use this book.

1. Each group member can be assigned some concepts or pages. During the group discussion, each member will summarize the sections, read the related Bible verses, and lead the discussions.
2. The group can simply start at the beginning and work their way through every section.
3. Personal experiences help to make the material come alive. Encourage group members to share related experiences. Ask questions to engage group members (i.e. "Did you know seaweed was mentioned in the Bible?").
4. Go to YouTube and find some short clips on the movies mentioned earlier. Share the scene with your group to tie biblical principles with current, real-life issues.
5. It is advisable to consider these three areas in each section being discussed:
    - Make sure the content is shared and understood (concept, quote, story, etc.).
    - Read the Bible verses. Discuss their application. Can group members suggest other further study?

- Read and discuss the Questions to Consider. Many of these questions are "What If" questions and should be thought-provoking for the group members.
- Make sure related experiences are shared with the group. You may not be a sea captain, but it is possible that you may be the head of your house or Sunday school class and had experiences with leadership, finances, salvation, etc.

BIBLIOGRAPHY

Arndt, W, F.W. Danker, W. Bauer, and F. Gingrich, F. *A Greek-English Lexicon of the New Testament and Other Early Christian Literature*, 3rd ed., Chicago: University of Chicago Press, 2000.

"Acts 5 Commentary." Precept Austin online. Updated May 14, 2022. https://www.preceptaustin.org/acts-5-commentary.

"Augustine of Hippo›Quotes›Quotable Quote." Goodreads.com. Accessed October 16, 2022. https://www.goodreads.com/quotes/721218-the-confession-of-evil-works-is-the-first-beginning-of.

Boom, Corrie ten, and Jamie Buckingham. *Tramp for the Lord*. Fort Washington, PA: CLC Publications, 2010.

Bergen, R.D. *1, 2 Samuel*. Vol. 7. Nashville: Broadman & Holman Publishers, 1996.

Cloud, Henry, and John Sims Townsend. *Boundaries: When to Say Yes, How to Say No to Take Control of Your Life*. Grand Rapids: Zondervan, 2017.

Clowney, Edmund P. *Bible Speaks Today: 1 Peter*. Vol. 18. Westmont: InterVarsity Press, 1988.

Comer, John Mark. *Ruthless Elimination of Hurry: How to Stay Emotionally Healthy and Spiritually Alive in Our Current Chaos, The*. London: Hodder & Stoughton, 2019.

Cymbala, Jim. *Spirit Rising: Tapping into the Power of the Holy Spirit*. Grand Rapids: Zondervan, 2014. Kindle Edition.

Edwards, Gene. *Tale of Three Kings: A Study in Brokenness, A.* Wheaton: Tyndale House Publishers, 1992.

Foster, Richard, and Kathryn A. Helmers. *Celebration of Discipline: The Path to Spiritual Growth.* London: Hodder, 2008.

Fee, Gordon D. *1 and 2 Timothy, Titus.* Grand Rapids: Baker Books, 2011.

Fee, Gordon D. *The First Epistle to the Corinthians.* Grand Rapids: Eerdmans Publishing Co. Kindle Edition.

"Franklin D. Roosevelt›Quotes›Quotable Quote." Goodreads.com. Accessed September 30, 2022, https://www.goodreads.com/quotes/1324527-a-smooth-sea-never-made-a-skilled-sailor.

Hillyer, Norman. *1 and 2 Peter, Jude.* Grand Rapids: Baker Books, 2011.

Jobes, Karen H. *Baker Exegetical Commentary on the New Testament: 1 Peter*, Vol. 21. Grand Rapids: Baker Academic, 2005.

Keller, Timothy. *Rediscovering Jonah: The Secret of God's Mercy.* New York City: Penguin Publishing Group, 2020. Kindle Edition.

Lewis, C.S. *Surprised by Joy: The Shape of My Early Life.* San Francisco: HarperOne, 2017.

Lewis, C.S. *Four Loves: The Much Beloved Exploration of the Nature of Love, The.* San Francisco: HarperOne, 2017.

MacDonald, George, and David L. Neuhouser. *George MacDonald: Selections from His Greatest Works.* New York: Victor Books, 1990.

Manning, Brennan. *Furious Longing of God, The.* Colorado Springs: David C. Cook, 2009.

Maxwell, John C. *21 Irrefutable Laws of Leadership: Follow Them and People Will Follow You, The*. New York: HarperCollins Leadership, 2022.

Maxwell, John C. *Developing the Leader Within You*. Nashville: Thomas Nelson, 2006.

Redpath, Alan. *Making of a Man of God: Lessons from the Life of David, The*. Grand Rapids, MI: Fleming H. Revell, 2004.

Reimer, Rob *Soul Care: 7 Transformational Principles for a Healthy Soul*. Franklin: Carpenter's Son Publishing, 2016.

Seiter, Courtney. "The Secret Psychology of Facebook: Why We Like, Share, Comment and Keep Coming Back." April 23, 2016. Buffer.com. https://buffer.com/resources/psychology-of-facebook.

Shein, Edgar. *Humble Inquiry: The Gentle Art of Asking Instead of Telling*. Oakland: Berrett-Koehler Publishers, 2013.

Simpson, A.B. *Days of Heaven Upon Earth*. Harrisburg: Christian Publishers, 1897.

Smith, B.K. and Page, F.S. *Amos, Obadiah, Jonah*, Vol. 19B Nashville: Broadman and Holman Publishers.

Tozer, A.W. *Pursuit of God, The*. Abbotsford: Aneko Press, 2015.

Tozer, A.W. *How to Be Filled with the Holy Spirit*. Chicago: Moody Publishing, 2016.

Tozer, A.W. and James L. Snyder. *Cloud by Day, a Fire by Night: Finding and Following God's Will for You, A*. Minneapolis: Bethany House Publishers, 2019.

Tozer, A.W., and James L. Snyder. *Tozer: The Mystery of the Holy Spirit*. Alachua: Bridge-Logos, 2007.

Tozer, A.W. and Ron Eggert. *Tozer for the Christian Leader: A 365-Day Devotional.* Chicago: Moody Publishers, 2015.

Tozer, A.W. and Warren W. Wiersbe. *Best of A.W. Tozer, The.* Camp Hill: WingSpread Publishers, 2007.

Walborn, Dr. Ron. "Session 1: The Garden Concept." Advanced Theological Seminary. May 27, 2016.YouTube video. 21:38. https://www.youtube.com/watch?v=TwFqaqkaUYw&list=PL34iKQ5Nuov1RDqTdgB1-lxlB7V7nX4qO&index=2.

Wiersbe, Warren. *Be Amazed (Minor Prophets): Restoring an Attitude of Wonder and Worship,* New York City: Victor Books.

Wiersbe, Warren W. *Be Determined: Standing Firm in the Face of Opposition: OT Commentary: Nehemiah.* Colorado Springs: David C. Cook, 2009.

Wiersbe, Warren W. *Bible Exposition Commentary, The: Matthew—Galatians.* Vol. 1. London: Victor Books, 1996.

Wiersbe, Warren. *The Bible Exposition Commentary.* Vol. 1. London: Victor Books, 1996.

Wilkes, C. Gene. *Jesus on Leadership.* Wheaton: Tyndale House Publishers, 1998.

Willard, Dallas. *Spirit of the Disciplines: Understanding How God Changes Lives, The.* San Francisco: HarperSanFrancisco, 1999.

"William Temple>Quotes>Quotable Quote," Goodreads.com, Accessed October 27, 2022, https://www.goodreads.com/quotes/441116-to-worship-is-to-quicken-the-conscience-by-the-holiness.

Ambassador International's mission is to magnify the Lord Jesus Christ and promote His Gospel through the written word.

We believe through the publication of Christian literature, Jesus Christ and His Word will be exalted, believers will be strengthened in their walk with Him, and the lost will be directed to Jesus Christ as the only way of salvation.

For more information about
AMBASSADOR INTERNATIONAL
please visit:

www.ambassador-international.com
@AmbassadorIntl
www.facebook.com/AmbassadorIntl

Thank you for reading this book. Please consider leaving us a review on your social media, favorite retailer's website, Goodreads or Bookbub, or our website.

MORE FROM AMBASSADOR INTERNATIONAL

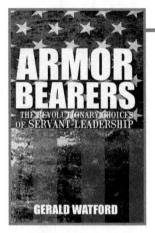

There is a desperate need for effective leadership today: in our nation, in our churches, in our families, and even in ourselves. The Bible uses the term *armorbearer* to describe leaders who offer help, support and strength to those around them. Packed with inspiring stories and powerful lessons, *Armorbearers* reveals the four revolutionary choices every leader must make, risking their own significance in order to encounter God in life-altering ways. Are you ready to become an armorbearer?

Whether you are an avid fisherman or don't know your floater from your line, *Theology of the Spring* can still awe and inspire you by bringing you back to the spring and, more importantly, to the One Who created the spring. Tapping into his love for fishing and the great outdoors, Pastor Jacob Taggart uses the spring to prove the existence, glory, and love of the Creator of all things. With vivid descriptions, Taggart paints a beautiful picture that will lure even the most reluctant participant to partake from the spring.

The devotions in *Called to Lead* are written for smart, hard-working, no-nonsense workplace leaders who are looking for something solid to help you improve your leadership. If you are looking for a devotional to simply warm your heart or cram more Scripture between your ears, find another book. If you are eager to close the gap between the leader you are and the leader God created you to be, humble enough to recognize that you could use some help, and willing to try a proven approach, invest a few minutes each week with this book pondering the intersection of your life and leadership and God's Word.

CPSIA information can be obtained
at www.ICGtesting.com
Printed in the USA
JSHW010034030423
39738JS00002B/44